PassKey
Learning Systems

EA Review: Part 2
Single Course Workbook

Three Complete
IRS Enrolled Agent Practice Exams
Businesses

May 1, 2022-February 28, 2023
Testing Cycle

D1725964

Joel Busch, CPA, JD
Christy Pinheiro, EA, ABA®
Thomas A. Gorczynski, EA, USTCP

Executive Editor: Joel Busch, CPA, JD

PassKey Learning Systems EA Review Part 2 Workbook: Three Complete IRS Enrolled Agent Practice Exams: Businesses (May 1, 2022-February 28, 2023 Testing Cycle)

ISBN 13: 978-1-935664-83-3

First Printing. April 1, 2022.

Cover images licensed with permission. Flag image ©Canva. Passport image ©2022 Moises Serrato Photography

PassKey EA Review® and PassKey Learning Systems® are U.S. Registered Trademarks.

Official website: *www.PassKeyOnline.com*

This workbook is designed for exam candidates who will take their EA exams in the May 1, 2022 to February 28, 2023 testing cycle.

Note: Prometric will NOT TEST on any legislation or court decisions passed after December 31, 2021. For exams taken between May 1, 2022 to February 28, 2023, all references on the examination are to the Internal Revenue Code, forms and publications, as amended through December 31, 2021. Also, unless otherwise stated, all questions relate to the calendar year 2021. Questions that contain the term 'current tax year' refer to the calendar year 2021.

This page intentionally left blank.

Table of Contents

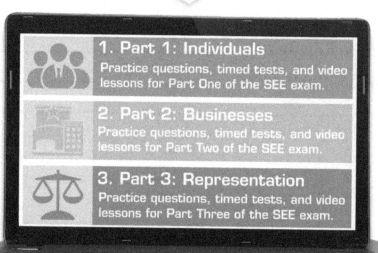

Recent Praise for the PassKey EA Review Series

(Real customers, real names, public testimonials)

I Highly recommend these materials
Tosha H. Knelangeon

Using only the [PassKey] study guide and the workbook, I passed all three EA exams on my first try. I highly recommend these materials. As long as you put in the time to read and study all the information provided, you should be well-prepared.

I passed on the first try.
Jake Bavaro

I recently passed the first part of the EA exam using just the textbook and a separate practice test workbook. The textbook is very easy to read and understand. Although I have a background in accounting and tax, someone with little or no knowledge of either should be able to grasp all of the various topics covered in the book. I really do believe that it is a superior preparation resource.

I passed all three parts my first time taking them.
Sheryl Reinecke

I passed all three parts the first time. I read each chapter and the review quiz at the end of each chapter. Before taking the real exam, I did the practice exams in the additional workbook. I feel the material adequately prepared me for success in passing the exam.

You can pass.
Vishnu Kali Osirion

I really rushed studying for this section. These authors make tax law relevant to your day-to-day experiences and understandable. You can pass the exam with just this as a resource. I do recommend purchasing the workbook as well, just for question exposure. The questions in the book and in the workbook are pretty indicative of what's on the exam. This is a must-buy. Cheers.

Suika Yutaka

I prefer self-study over any other type of course, and I loved this book. I have a very demanding job, and this made me greatly appreciate the concise and to-the-point style of this book. Also, note that this is the most reasonably priced full review (i.e., covering all three parts of the exam) I know of. Greatest praise!

Sharlene D.
Absolute Best Purchase

This book was definitely worth the purchase. The layout was great, especially the examples! Reading the book from front to back allowed me to pass [Part 2]. I also recommend purchasing the workbook or subscribing to the material on their website for this section.

Excellent explanations!
Janet Briggs

The best thing about these books is that each answer has a comprehensive explanation about why the answer is correct. I passed all three EA exams on the first attempt.

PassKey was the only study aid that I used
Stephen J Woodard, CFP, CLU, ChFC

The [PassKey] guides were an invaluable resource. They were concise and covered the subject matter succinctly with spot-on end-of-chapter questions that were very similar to what I encountered on the exams.

Amazing!
Sopio Svanishvilion

PassKey helped me pass all three parts of the Enrolled Agent exam. They are a "must-have" if you want to pass your EA exams.

I passed all three with Passkey.
Swathi B.R.

I went through the online membership, read the whole book, solved all the questions, and passed the EA exam on my first attempt. For all three [parts], I referred to Passkey EA Review. Wonderful books.

Very useful, I passed my exams by reading only PassKey!
Shixiong Feng

Very useful, I passed the 1st and 2nd exams by only reading the PassKey EA Review. If you are willing to spend some time reading the whole book thoroughly, then this book is the only thing you need to pass the EA exams.

A great EA review book
William Highfield (Lafayette, Colorado)

I used the Passkey EA Review book as a study guide and passed all my tests the first time. Don't get the idea the tests were easy, but the book was so well-organized and inclusive that the memorization and familiarization processes went very well.

This review is the best on the market.
Yaw Asiante-Asamoah

I passed on all three parts in one attempt. The questions in the Review and Workbook are similar to the real exams. I got a big raise, and my bonus went up at my seasonal job. It's worth the money, trust me.

Outstanding Material!
E. De La Garza

If you're looking to pass the EA exam with minimal expense, I recommend the PassKey system.

Introduction

This PassKey EA Review Businesses Workbook is designed to accompany the PassKey EA Review study guide for Businesses, which presents a comprehensive overview of the material you must learn to pass part 2 of the IRS Special Enrollment Exam (SEE), commonly called the EA exam. This workbook features three complete enrolled agent practice exams, specifically created for the EA exam cycle that runs from May 1, 2022 to February 28, 2023.

Each sample exam has 100 questions, similar to the ones you will encounter when you take your actual exam. These test questions are all unique and not found in the PassKey study guides. This is intentional, so EA candidates can have a more true-to-life test-taking experience when they go through the workbook questions.

Any EA exam candidate will benefit from the exam questions and detailed answers in this workbook. We suggest that you use it as a study tool to prepare for the exam in a realistic setting. Set aside an uninterrupted block of time and test yourself, just as you would if you were actually taking the EA exam at a testing center.

Score yourself at the end, and then review the answers carefully. Unlike the Prometric exam, you will have a complete, clear answer for each question. If you miss a question, you will know why. Use this workbook to uncover your weak points and concentrate on improving in those areas. You should answer at least 80% of the questions correctly. Any score below 80% means you need to study more.

All of the questions in the workbook are based on 2021 tax law, which corresponds with the current EA exam cycle. If you have any questions about the actual exam or if you want to sign up for it, go directly to the Prometric website at *www.prometric.com/IRS*. If you would like to find out more about the PassKey EA Review study program and other learning products by PassKey Publications, visit our website at *www.passkeyonline.com*.

Successfully passing the EA exam can launch you into a fulfilling and lucrative new career. The exam requires intense preparation and diligence, but with the help of PassKey's EA Review, you will have the tools you need to learn how to become an enrolled agent.

As the authors of the PassKey EA Review, we wish you much success.

This page intentionally left blank.

Essential Tax Law Figures for Businesses

Here is a quick summary of some of the essential tax figures for the revised enrolled agent exam cycle (May 1, 2022 to February 28, 2023).

Important Legislation for the 2021 Tax Year

- The *American Rescue Plan Act of 2021 (ARPA)* was signed into law on March 11, 2021, by President Biden. This bill included dozens of tax provisions that affect individuals and businesses in the 2021 tax year.
- The *Infrastructure Investment and Jobs Act of 2021 (IIJA)* was signed on November 15, 2021, by President Biden. Most of the provisions in the bill were designed to stimulate infrastructure spending, but there were some business tax provisions included. The IIJA includes provisions to extend the time for filing a petition with the U.S. Tax Court and expands the definition of brokers to include businesses that regularly transfer digital assets (cryptocurrency) on behalf of another person.
- The *Consolidated Appropriations Act, 2021 (CAA 2021)* was signed into law on December 27, 2020, by President Trump. This legislation extended and modified many provisions of the earlier CARES Act.

2021 General Filing Deadlines

If a due date falls on a weekend or legal holiday, the deadline is pushed to the next business day.

- **Individual filing deadline:** April 18, 2022 (extended due date: October 17, 2022).[1]
- **Estates and Trusts Income Tax Return Deadline (Form 1041):** April 18, 2022 (extension period of 5½ months; due September 30 for a calendar-year entity).
- **Estate Tax Return Deadline (Form 706):** Due within nine months after the date of the decedent's death (a 6-month extension is available).
- **Partnership Deadline (Form 1065):** March 15, 2022 (extended due date: September 15, 2022), or the 15th day of the 3rd month after the end of the partnership's tax year, for fiscal-year filers.
- **C Corporation Deadline (Form 1120):** April 18, 2022 (extended due date: October 17, 2022), or the 15th day of the fourth month following the end of the corporation's tax year, in the case of most fiscal-year filers.
- **C Corporations with a June 30th Fiscal Year End:** Due the 15th day of the 3rd month after the end of the entity's tax year. For a June 30 fiscal year entity, Form 1120 is due September 15th with an extended due date of April 15 the *following* year.
- **S Corporation Deadline (Form 1120-S):** March 15, 2022 (extended due date: September 15, 2022) or by the 15th day of the 3rd month following the end of the tax year for fiscal year filers.

---

[1] Taxpayers will have until April 18, 2022, to file their 2021 return because of the Emancipation Day holiday in the District of Columbia. Taxpayers in Maine and Massachusetts will have until April 19, 2022, because of the Patriots' Day holiday in those states. The extended deadline is October 17, 2022, because October 15 falls on a Saturday in 2022.

- **Exempt Entity Deadline (Form 990):** May 15 for a calendar-year exempt entity (extended due date: November 15).
- **Employee benefit plan (Form 5500 series):** Due the last day of the 7th calendar month after the end of the plan's tax year; July 31 for a calendar-year plan (an extension is available to October 15 for a calendar-year plan).
- **FBAR:** The official due date for the FBAR (FinCen 114) coincides with the filing of the federal tax return (normally April 15). However, an automatic extension is allowed until October 15.[2]

Estimated Tax Due Dates:

- **Individuals:** Quarterly estimated taxes are due by April 15, June 15, September 15, and January 15 of the following year.
- **Farmers and Fishermen:** January 15 (if *not* filing a return by March 1), or March 1 (if filing a tax return on or before Mar 1).
- **Corporations**: April 15, June 15, September 15, and December 15 (for calendar-year corporations).

Form 1099 Deadlines: The deadline for distributing 1099s and W-2s to the payees: January 31.

> **Note:** A 30-day extension may be requested for information returns. For Forms W-2 and 1099-NEC, an extension is only allowed for *extraordinary* circumstances, such as in the case of a natural disaster, death of the business owner, or other extraordinary events. Form 8809 is used to request an extension.

"Perfection Periods" for Rejected Submissions: The IRS provides a "transmission perfection period" for rejected returns. Individual returns are given a 5-day perfection period, while most business returns are given a 10-day perfection period; however, the Transmission Perfection Period for an extension to file Form 4868, 7004, or 8868 is 5 days.

2021 Maximum Compensation Subject to FICA

- OASDI[3] maximum wage base: $142,800
- Employee: 7.65% (6.2% Social Security + 1.45% Medicare)
- Employer: 7.65% (6.2% Social Security + 1.45% Medicare)
- Self-employed 15.30% (12.4% Social Security + 2.9% Medicare)
- Maximum FICA/SE Tax: Employee: $8,853.60, Self-employed: $17,707.20, Medicare: No limit
- **Additional Medicare Tax:** 0.9% on earned income exceeding the following thresholds:
  - Married filing jointly: $250,000
  - Married filing separately: $125,000
  - Single, HOH and QW: $200,000

---

[2] FBAR refers to Form 114, Report of Foreign Bank and Financial Accounts, that must be filed with the Financial Crimes Enforcement Network (FinCEN), which is a bureau of the Treasury Department. Although the FBAR is not filed directly with the IRS, the IRS is responsible for FBAR enforcement.

[3] "OASDI" is the official name for Social Security in the United States, and the terms are often used interchangeably. The acronym stands for "Old-Age, Survivors, and Disability Insurance."

2021 FUTA Wage Base: The FUTA tax rate is 6% on the first $7,000 paid to each employee. Only the employer pays FUTA tax. The tax is not withheld from the employee's wages.

2021 Net Investment Income Tax (NIIT): The tax is 3.8% of the *lesser* of:
- Net investment income, or
- The amount of modified adjusted gross income (MAGI) over $13,050 for Estates and trusts.

2021 "Nanny Tax" on Household Employees: The nanny tax threshold is $2,300 in 2021. A household employer is normally obligated to withhold and pay federal FICA (Social Security and Medicare) taxes for any household employee they paid $2,300 or more during the year. A household employer is required to pay FUTA taxes if they paid a household employee $1,000 or more in a calendar quarter in the current or prior year. These thresholds are on a *per-employee* basis.

2021 Estate and Trust *Exemption* Amounts
- Estate Exemption Amount: $600
- Simple Trust: $300
- Complex Trust: $100
- Qualified disability trusts: $4,300

2021 Estate and Gift Tax *Exclusion* Amounts

- Estate and gift tax (highest rate): 40%
- Estate tax exemption: $11,700,000
- Lifetime gift/GST exemption: $11,700,000
- Gift tax annual exclusion: $15,000
- Annual exclusion for gifts to noncitizen spouse: $159,000

2021 QSEHRA Limits (Maximum payments and reimbursements through the QSEHRA):
- $5,300 for the employee only; or
- $10,700 for an employee plus family members of the employee

2021 FSA Limits:
- **Dependent Care FSA (DCFSA):** up to $10,500 in 2021 only ($5,250 for MFS filers). Employers can adopt this change to their benefit plans and make it effective for all of 2021, if the plan amendments are in place before the last day of the plan's year.
- **Health Care FSA (HCFSA):** $2,750. ARPA did not increase the dependent care FSA contribution limits for 2021.
- **Carryover of unused amounts:** As part of the disaster relief provisions implemented by the CAA 2021, employers may allow participants to carryover unused benefits or contributions remaining in an FSA from 2021 to 2022. These provisions are optional and employers are not required to adopt them.

2021 HSA and HDHP Limits: To qualify to contribute to a health savings account, the taxpayer must have a high-deductible health insurance policy. The plan must also have an annual limit on out-of-pocket expenses (not including premiums).[4]

HSA Contribution maximum	Self-only: $3,600, Family: $7,200
HDHP minimum deductible	Self-only: $1,400, Family: $2,800
HDHP maximum out-of-pocket amounts (not including insurance premiums)	Self-only: $7,000, Family: $14,000
HSA catch-up contributions (age 55 or older)	$1,000

2021 Contribution Limits – Retirement Plans

- **Roth and traditional IRAs:** $6,000 (additional catch-up contribution of $1,000 for taxpayers age 50 or older)
- **Roth IRA contribution limit phaseout (MAGI):**
  - $125,000 to $140,000 – Single and HOH
  - $198,000 to $208,000 – Married filing jointly
  - $0 to $10,000 – Married filing separately (lived with spouse)[5]
- **401(k) /403(b) plan Employee Salary Deferral Limits:** $19,500 ($6,500 catch-up)
- **SEP-IRA contribution limits (employee + employer):** Up to 25% of compensation, up to a maximum contribution of $58,000[6] SEP-IRA contributions can be made up to the due date of the return, *including* extensions.
- **SIMPLE IRA and SIMPLE 401(k) limits:** Under age 50: $13,500; (50 and over: $16,500)
- **Qualified plan contribution limits:** The limit on annual benefits for a participant in a defined benefit plan is $230,000 for 2021.:[7]

2021 Section 179 Expense

- Maximum deduction amount: $1,050,000
- Beginning phaseout limitation: $2,620,000
- Spending cap: $3,670,000
- Heavy SUV Limit: $26,200

---

[4] An HSA can be combined with a qualified high-deductible health plan and offers the opportunity to save for health care on a pre-tax basis. Another name for an HDHP is an "HSA-Eligible" Plan.

[5] With regards to the Roth contribution limit, if the taxpayer is "married filing separately" but did not live with their spouse at any time during the year, the taxpayer may use the higher phaseout threshold for single taxpayers.

[6] SEP-IRAs do not allow catch up contributions. They still apply to SARSEPs, and older, similar type of plan. No new SARSEPs were allowed after 1996, but grandfathered SARSEPs still exist.

[7] A defined benefit plan is also called a "traditional pension" and these retirement plans are solely funded by the employer, not the employee. Actuarial assumptions and computations are required to figure these contributions.

2021 Bonus Depreciation:

The 100% bonus depreciation amount remains in effect through January 1, 2023. Bonus depreciation also applies to used property. Assets that qualify for bonus depreciation include:

- MACRS property with a recovery period of 20 years or less
- Computer software
- Water utility property
- Land improvements
- Qualified improvement property
- Qualified film or television production (excluding pornographic films)
- Qualified live theatrical production, as defined in section 181(e)
- Fruit and nut-bearing trees[8]

2021 QBI deduction Limits

The qualified business income (QBI) deduction is up to 20% of QBI from a pass-through entity conducting a trade or business in the U.S. It also includes up to 20% of qualified real estate investment trust (REIT) dividends and qualified publicly traded partnership (PTP) income. Certain limitations may reduce or eliminate the deduction amount. The Section 199A limitation phase-in ranges are as follows and are based on taxable income:

- Married filing jointly: $329,800-$429,800
- Head of Household/QW/Single: $164,900-$214,900
- Married filing Separately: $164,925-$214,925

2021 Standard Mileage Rates:

- Business: 56¢ per mile
- Charitable purposes: 14¢ per mile
- Medical and moving: 16¢ per mile

2021 Qualified Transportation Benefits:[9]

- Commuter benefits/transit passes: $270 per month.
- Parking: $270 per month.

---

[8] This includes grapevines, orange trees, almonds and olive orchards, etc. In the past, fruit and nut bearing trees would not be "placed in service" for several years, because the trees would not be "placed in service" until they bear fruit. Now, farmers are allowed to take bonus depreciation at the time of planting. This is an election for bonus depreciation only. These plants and trees would not be eligible for Section 179 in their pre-productive period. A farmer may also choose to wait, and when the trees begin bearing fruit or nuts, then the farmer may claim section 179 or regular MACRS depreciation.

[9] The transportation benefits are excluded from W-2 wages, but the business itself is no longer allowed a deduction for the expense.

Tax Law Updates for Businesses

New Schedules K-2 and K-3: These Schedules are new for the 2021 tax year. Schedules K-2 and K-3 are required by partnerships and S corporations with items of international tax relevance. Both schedules include foreign reportable items. The form details are as follows:

- **Form 1065 (Schedule K-2)** *Partner's Distributive Share Items—International*

- **Form 1065 (Schedule K-3)** *Partner's Share of Income, Deductions, Credits, etc.—International*

- **Form 1120-S (Schedule K-2)** *Shareholders Pro Rata Share Items—International*

- **Form 1120-S (Schedule K-3)** *Shareholder's Share of Income, Deductions, Credits, etc.—International*

There has been some confusion about these new foreign reporting requirements. As a response, on February 16, 2022, the IRS issued Notice 2021-39, offering transitional penalty relief to partnerships that make a good faith effort to comply with the new reporting requirement. E-filing of these forms will be delayed as the IRS attempts to catch up its computer system to accept these new forms. E-filing for the new Schedules K-2 and K-3 will not be available until the following dates:

- March 20, 2022, for Form 1065

- Mid-June 2022, for Form 1120-S

PPP Loan Forgiveness: The U.S. Small Business Administration's Paycheck Protection Program (PPP) forgiven loans are excluded from gross income. The business expenses paid with loan proceeds can still be deducted.

Economic Injury Disaster Assistance (EIDL) Loans and Advances: The CAA-2021 Act allows Economic Injury Disaster Assistance (EIDL) Advances provided as emergency grants under the CARES Act to be excluded from gross income while the corresponding expenses would remain deductible. The CAA-2021 clarifies that any loan forgiveness granted to an EIDL loan recipient under discretionary powers provided by the CARES Act does not result in gross income or a denial of deductions for allocable expenses.[10]

2021 Meal Deduction Rules: Businesses, including self-employed taxpayers, may claim 100% of food or beverage expenses paid to restaurants. Under this temporary provision, "restaurants" include businesses that prepare and sell food or beverages to retail customers for immediate on-premises and/or off-premises consumption. On November 16, 2021, the Internal Revenue Service issued Notice 2021-63, clarifying that the 100% meal expense deduction also applies to the meal portion of a per diem rate or allowance. Business meals purchased at any other setting or venue are still subject to the 50% limitation.

---

[10] The CAA 2021 repealed Section 1110(e)(6) of the CARES Act that required PPP loan forgiveness to be reduced by any EIDL advances (up to $10,000). This retroactive provision will allow any PPP borrowers who had forgiveness reduced by EIDL advances to have it forgiven.

Social Security Tax Deferral: The CARES Act gave businesses and household employers the option to delay deposits of the employer portion of the Social Security tax between March 27, 2020 and December 31, 2020. This was a *deferral*, not a *forgiveness*, and the Act stipulated that half of the taxes be paid by December 31, 2021, and the other half by December 31, 2022. Prior to the 2021 payment deadline, employers should have received an IRS notice of the amount owed.

Net Operating Losses: NOLs arising in tax year 2021 and beyond may only be carried forward. A NOL deduction cannot exceed more than 80% of taxable income. Losses generated prior to 2018 are not subject to the 80% limitation. An NOL may be carried forward indefinitely until the loss is used up or the taxpayer dies. For pass-through entities (partnerships and S corporations), the excess loss limit applies at the partner and shareholder level.

- **Farmer exception:** noncorporate farming businesses have a 2-year carryback. An election may be made to waive the carryback period. If an NOL consists of both a farming loss and a non-farming loss, the losses should be treated separately. The farming loss is treated as a separate NOL and taken into account only after the non-farming NOL is applied.

- **Exception for casualty insurance companies:** property and casualty insurance companies[11] are allowed a 2-year carryback period for NOLs. An election may be made to waive the carryback period. These companies' NOL carryforward is limited to 20 years and the 80% limitation does not apply.

- **Excess Business Loss Limitations:** For 2021 through 2026, excess business losses of *noncorporate* taxpayers are subject to an annual limit of $262,000 for individual taxpayers and $524,000 for married taxpayers filing jointly.[12] Excess losses over these amounts must be carried forward. Excess business losses that are disallowed are treated as a net operating loss carryover to the following taxable year.

Stalled Efile Mandates for Businesses: The Taxpayer First Act of 2019, enacted July 1, 2019, authorized the IRS to issue regulations that would reduce the aggregate number of information returns that would trigger a mandatory efile requirement for most businesses from 250 to 100 for returns required to be filed in 2022, and then to 10 returns for processing years after 2022. Proposed regulations were released July 21, 2021, but no additional guidance from the IRS was forthcoming.

Applications for nonprofit exemption: After April 5, 2021, organizations must electronically file Form 1024-A through Pay.gov. Form 1024-A is used for organizations seeking to be exempt under Section 501(c)(4). The required user fee for Form 1024 is $600 for 2021.

---

[11] This special rule applies to insurance companies other than life insurance companies.

[12] Losses from sales or exchanges of capital assets are not included in the calculation of the total deductions from a taxpayer's trades or businesses. Losses from a farming business must apply the excess business loss limitation before carrying any NOLs back 2 years.

This page intentionally left blank.

Part 1: Business Practice Exams

Test Tip: Time yourself. Set up a watch or other digital timer while you read and answer the questions. You will have 3.5 hours to take Part 2 of the EA exam - Businesses - with approximately two minutes to answer each question. Don't spend an inordinate amount of time on any one question and make sure to answer each one, even if you're not sure of the right answer. All questions left blank are counted as wrong on the EA exam.

This page intentionally left blank.

#1 Sample Exam: Businesses

(Please test yourself first, then check the correct answers at the end of this exam.)

1. Brielle is the owner of Honeywell Tax Services, a sole proprietorship. The business has gross receipts of $11,253 and supply expenses of $3,175 in 2021. Brielle also paid $4,200 for self-employed health insurance during the year. Brielle uses her own car for business. Her written mileage log shows she drove 1,200 business-related miles during the year. She uses the standard mileage rate to determine her driving expenses. Based on this information, what is the total of her allowable business deductions on Schedule C?

A. $654
B. $3,847
C. $7,375
D. $8,029

2. When does a decedent's estate cease to exist?

A. When it is insolvent.
B. When the beneficiaries terminate the estate in probate court.
C. When the executor steps down or resigns.
D. When all of the estate's assets are distributed.

3. On January 1, 2021, Elsewise Partnership, a calendar-year, cash-basis business, purchased a liability insurance policy for its business. The policy period is for three full years and is required to be paid in advance the first year. Elsewise Partnership pays $1,800 for the policy. How much of this policy is deductible in 2021?

A. $180
B. $450
C. $600
D. $1,800

4. Jiro is a partner in Agro-Growers, LLC, which is taxed as a partnership. At the end of the year, Jiro's adjusted basis in Agro-Growers was $65,000. Jiro received a nonliquidating distribution of land from Agro-Growers, as well as $15,000 of cash. The land had an adjusted basis of $65,000 to Agro-Growers and a fair market value of $54,000 immediately before the distribution. What is Jiro's basis in the land after the distribution?

A. $44,000
B. $50,000
C. $54,000
D. $65,000

5. Which of the following statements is correct regarding a husband and wife who own and run an unincorporated business together, with each spouse materially participating in the business?

A. A married couple can choose to report their business as a sole proprietorship by electing to file as a qualified joint venture and filing two separate Schedules C and two Schedules SE. They must file jointly.
B. A married couple can choose to report their business as a sole proprietorship by electing to file as a qualified joint venture and filing a single Schedule C and a single Schedule SE. They must file jointly.
C. A married couple cannot operate a partnership together.
D. A married couple can elect to be treated as a single individual for Social Security tax purposes.

6. The Perdue Trust has $45,000 in investment income during the year. All the income is distributed to three 501(c)(3) charities and one political organization. What form must be used to report the trust's income?

A. Form 709
B. Form 990
C. Form 1041
D. No filings are required.

7. All of the following types of entities must be taxed as a corporation *except*:

A. An insurance company.
B. A joint-stock association.
C. A business owned by a state or local government.
D. A business with annual gross receipts of $100 million or more.

8. Cheryl is a 100% shareholder in Sterling Design, Inc. a cash-basis C corporation. At the beginning of the year, Sterling Design had no accumulated earnings and profits. At the end of the year, Sterling Design has $20,000 of current and accumulated earnings and profits. Sterling Design makes a $30,000 cash distribution to Cheryl. At the time of the distribution, Cheryl's stock basis in the corporation was $0. What is the effect of this distribution?

A. $30,000 taxable dividend.
B. $20,000 taxable dividend; $10,000 capital gain.
C. $20,000 taxable dividend; $10,000 capital loss.
D. $30,000 capital gain.

9. In which of the following scenarios is a fiduciary required to file a Form 1041 for a U.S. trust?

A. A trust that has $100 in taxable income for the year.
B. Nontaxable municipal bond interest income of $900.
C. A trust that has a beneficiary who is a nonresident alien.
D. All of the above.

10. Broadpoint, Inc. is an accrual-based C corporation. Broadpoint, Inc. realized net income of $300,000 for book purposes in 2021. Included in *book* net income are the following:

Federal income taxes	$4,000
Excess of capital losses over capital gains	10,000
Tax-exempt interest income	5,000

What is Broadpoint, Inc.'s taxable income?

A. $280,000
B. $290,000
C. $304,000
D. $309,000

11. The Jones Family Trust is an irrevocable trust that has an annual filing requirement. The entity has a fiscal year-end of May 30. When is the trust's income tax return (Form 1041) due?

A. April 15
B. August 15
C. September 15
D. November 15

12. Allwise Corporation makes a $100,000 term loan to one of its shareholders. The stated principal amount of the loan is payable in ten years. The test rate used to determine if the loan is a below-market loan is the:

A. Short-term applicable Federal rate as of the day the loan is made.
B. Mid-term applicable Federal rate as of the day the loan is made.
C. Long-term applicable Federal rate as of the day the loan is made.
D. Adjusted applicable Federal rate as of the day the loan is made.

13. Fancy Flowers, LLC is a cash-basis business, taxed as a partnership with two members. During the year, Fancy Flowers paid $30 a month to a local church for a half-page advertisement in its monthly program for funerary and bridal flower bouquets. The purpose of the ad was to encourage the church's parishioners to buy their flower arrangements and bouquets from Fancy Flowers. How should Fancy Flowers, LLC treat this transaction on their Form 1065, *Partnership Return?*

A. Unreimbursed partnership expense.
B. Advertising expense.
C. Charitable donation.
D. Nondeductible expense.

14. Which of the following is a *benefit* that a C corporation has over an S corporation?

A. Potential double taxation on earnings.
B. Corporate losses to pass through to shareholders.
C. Deductible charitable contributions at the business entity level.
D. Liability protection.

15. What is a "closely-held" corporation?

A. A corporation with less than 100 shareholders.
B. Another name for an S corporation.
C. A corporation with assets of less than $10 million.
D. A corporation with a small number of shareholders and no public market for its corporate stock.

16. Elaine operates a comic book store and reports her income on Schedule C. Elaine hires her 16-year-old son, Devin, part-time to help her run the store. Elaine pays her son a reasonable wage of $12,900 for the year. Which of the following statements is correct about Devin's wages?

A. Elaine may deduct Devin's wages as a business expense, and the wages are not subject to Social Security and Medicare taxes.
B. Elaine cannot deduct the wages she paid to Devin, and the wages are subject to the kiddie tax.
C. Elaine cannot deduct the wages she paid to Devin because of related party transaction rules.
D. Elaine may deduct Devin's wages as a business expense, and the wages are subject to Social Security and Medicare taxes.

17. Which of the following is a correct statement about sales tax collected by a business in connection with the sale of goods or services in a state which imposes sales tax on the buyers of goods or services and the seller is required to collect and remit the taxes on behalf of the state?

A. A business may deduct sales taxes collected in the year they are remitted to the taxing authorities.
B. Sales taxes collected are deducted from gross receipts.
C. Sales taxes are excluded from gross receipts and deductible expenses.
D. Sales taxes collected are added to gross receipts.

18. Sherry is a self-employed financial planner who files a Schedule C. In which of the following instances would Sherry *not* be required to obtain an employer identification number (EIN)?

A. Sherry hires an employee.
B. Sherry forms a partnership with her husband.
C. Sherry operates multiple sole proprietorships, each with no employees.
D. Sherry files for bankruptcy under Chapter 7.

19. Lance is a medical doctor and the sole shareholder of Estyle Aesthetics, Inc., a plastic surgery clinic organized as a C corporation. For 2021 Lance received $185,000 in wages from the clinic, which is reasonable compensation for a plastic surgeon in his area. Another $350,000 in wages was paid to the clinic's other employees. After deducting expenses, Estyle Aesthetics, Inc. has $90,000 of income from operations, and an additional $80,000 of long-term capital gain, resulting in taxable income of $170,000. Based on this information, what is Estyle Aesthetics' section 199A qualified business income (QBI) deduction for 2021?

A. $0
B. $14,000
C. $18,000
D. $34,000

20. Gabby owns a duplex. She lives in one half and rents the other to a tenant. On January 13, 2021, the property was condemned by the government in order to build a public light rail system. Gabby receives a condemnation settlement from the government of $90,000. She originally paid $75,000 for the property and spent $15,000 for substantial improvements equally on the two units. Gabby had claimed allowable depreciation deductions of $20,000 on the rental half of the property before the condemnation. She also incurred legal fees of $2,000 in connection with the condemnation settlement process. She doesn't plan to purchase another property; she just takes the settlement and puts it in her savings account. What amount of taxable gain (or loss) will Gabby report as a result of the condemnation assuming she does not defer any gain under section 1033?

A. Taxable gain of $0.
B. Taxable gain of $19,000.
C. Deductible loss of $2,000.
D. Deductible loss of $22,000.

21. Dominion Services, Inc. is a calendar-year C corporation that uses the accrual method of accounting. As of December 20, 2021, Dominion Services, Inc. had earned and was entitled to receive $22,000 in connection with a service contract. Dominion Services, Inc. received payment for half of the contract ($11,000) on December 29, 2021. However, Dominion Services, Inc. did not receive payment for the remainder of the contract from its customer until January 3, 2022. The company did not cash either check until January 10, 2022. How much should the company report on its tax return for this transaction, and when should the amounts be reported?

A. $22,000 in 2022.
B. $22,000 in 2021.
C. $11,000 in 2021 and $11,000 in 2022.
D. $22,000 in 2021 or in 2022 by election.

22. The Dunne Corporation is a calendar-year C corporation. In 2021, Dunne Corp. made $4,000 in charitable contributions that it cannot use on the current-year return because of income limitations. How should this unused contribution be treated?

A. The corporation can carry forward unused charitable contributions for 10 years.
B. The corporation can carry forward unused charitable contributions for 20 years.
C. The corporation can carry forward unused charitable contributions for five years.
D. The corporation can carry forward unused contributions indefinitely.

23. Riaan transfers an office building to Delphi Corporation in exchange for 70% of its outstanding stock; no one else received stock in the transaction. Prior to the contribution, Riaan does not own any stock in Delphi Corporation. The office building had an adjusted basis of $125,000 to Riaan and an FMV of $300,000. The corporate stock that Riaan receives in the transfer has an FMV of $300,000. How much gain or loss would Riaan recognize in this transfer?

A. $0.
B. $175,000 gain.
C. $175,000 loss.
D. $300,000 gain.

24. In which of the following situations is a business not required to request a *new* employer identification number (EIN)?

A. When a taxpayer dies, and a taxable estate is created.
B. When a sole proprietor files for bankruptcy under Chapter 7 or Chapter 11.
C. When an existing corporation establishes a pension plan.
D. When a sole proprietor adds an additional location to his business.

25. Which of the following types of trusts generally does not have to file an annual tax return?

A. An irrevocable trust.
B. A revocable grantor trust.
C. A qualified disability trust.
D. A charitable trust that is formed as a private foundation.

26. Which entity type has an annual filing requirement, regardless of its level of income or expenses?

A. Exempt entity
B. Corporation
C. Partnership
D. Estate

27. Christian is a 50% general partner in Copperleaf Partnership. On January 1, 2021, Christian's partnership basis was $1,000. Copperleaf Partnership had the following items of income, calculated at the end of the year:

Ordinary income	$40,000
Tax-exempt investment income	20,000
Rental income	4,000

There were no distributions to any of the partners during the year. Based on this information, what is Christian's partnership basis on December 31, 2021?

A. $21,000
B. $22,000
C. $23,000
D. $33,000

28. Patricia is a sole proprietor with three employees. She has been in business for six years, and she reports her business income on Schedule C. She wants to set up a new SIMPLE IRA for herself and her three employees. She has never had any type of retirement plan for her business. What is the final deadline for her to set up a SIMPLE IRA for the 2021 tax year?

A. October 1, 2021
B. December 31, 2021
C. January 1, 2022
D. March 15, 2022

29. Section 1245 generally does not apply to:

A. Depreciable personal property.
B. Livestock held for the production of income.
C. Machinery or equipment used in a business.
D. Real property.

30. Roger is a driver for a popular rideshare service, Lite-Car Rideshare. He works as an independent contractor and files Schedule C. Roger uses his own car to work for the rideshare service and tracks his business mileage using an application on his cellphone. In 2021, he put a total of 15,000 miles on his car, 6,800 of which were for Lite-Car Rideshare. He decides to take the standard mileage rate. What is his deduction for mileage on Schedule C?

A. $2,500
B. $3,808
C. $3,944
D. $8,400

31. Which of the following is considered a "pass-through" entity?

A. A C corporation.
B. A tax-exempt organization.
C. An S corporation.
D. A qualified retirement plan.

32. Treeland Nursery is a wholesale plant nursery that sells trees and shrubs for commercial landscaping. Treeland Nursery purchased a large greenhouse for $125,000 several years ago. It is a single-purpose agricultural structure, so it is Section 1245 property. Treeland Nursery has taken depreciation deductions of $39,000, and the adjusted basis in the greenhouse is $86,000 when Treeland Nursery sells it on December 10, 2021, for $180,000. What is the nature and amount of Treeland Nursery's gain or loss from the sale?

A. Capital gain of $94,000.
B. Ordinary income of $94,000.
C. Ordinary income of $39,000 and a capital gain of $55,000.
D. Capital gain income of $39,000 and ordinary income of $55,000.

33. Bruce paid $5,500 for a new commercial drill press for his construction business. The shipping cost was $125. When the machine arrived, it was too difficult for Bruce to assemble and install himself, so he paid a professional to set up the machine for a cost of $250. What is Bruce's adjusted basis in this asset?

A. $5,125
B. $5,550
C. $5,625
D. $5,875

34. Which of the following would make a corporation *ineligible* to elect S corporation status?

A. One shareholder is a bankruptcy estate.
B. One shareholder is a partnership.
C. The corporation has both voting and nonvoting stock.
D. The corporation has 100 shareholders.

35. What is the accumulated earnings tax?

A. A 20% tax that is assessed on the excess accumulated earnings and profits of a C corporation.
B. A 20% tax that is assessed on the excess accumulated earnings and profits of an S corporation.
C. A 15% tax that is imposed upon the undistributed income of an estate.
D. A 15% excise tax that is imposed in addition to the trust fund recovery penalty.

36. Montana Equine Rescue is a 501(c)(3) exempt entity that is organized as a calendar-year corporation. What is the normal (unextended) due date of Montana Equine Rescue's tax return, and which form number is it required to file?

Form Number	**Due Date**
A. Form 1120	April 15
B. Form 990	April 15
C. Form 1120	May 15
D. Form 990	May 15

37. Microproducts Inc. is a cash-basis C corporation. During the year, the corporation pays $1,000,000 in salary to Colson, its sole employee-shareholder. The following year, Microproducts Inc. is audited by the IRS, and Colson's salary is deemed to be excessive. In this case, the excessive part of the salary will normally be treated as a:

A. Constructive distribution.
B. Liquidating distribution.
C. Prohibited transaction.
D. Nontaxable distribution.

38. Yasmin and Kerry formed Bohme Coffeehouse, LLC during the year. For tax purposes, Bohme Coffeehouse is treated as a partnership. Yasmin contributes $32,000 of cash. Kerry contributes $10,000 of cash and a used delivery truck with an FMV of $40,000 and an adjusted basis of $18,000. Yasmin and Kerry are equal partners (50/50) in the partnership. What is *Kerry's* basis in her partnership interest *after* her contribution?

A. $10,000
B. $28,000
C. $32,000
D. $50,000

39. What does an S corporation's *accumulated adjustments account* (AAA) include?

A. All items of income and expenses of the S corporation.
B. All items of income and expenses of the S corporation with the exception of portfolio income (and expenses related to portfolio income).
C. All items of income and expenses of the S corporation with the exception of tax-exempt income (and expenses related to tax-exempt income).
D. An accounting of each shareholder's stock basis in the corporation and related adjustments of foreign shareholders.

40. Christopher is the sole shareholder of Alliance Brokers, Inc., a calendar-year C corporation. At the beginning of the year, Alliance Brokers has accumulated earnings and profits of $150,000. On September 1, the corporation distributes $200,000 to Christopher in a nonliquidating distribution. At the time of the distribution, his stock basis is $30,000. Alliance Brokers has no additional earnings and profits during the year. How should Christopher recognize this $200,000 distribution on his return?

A. He must recognize dividend income of $150,000 and a taxable capital gain of $20,000. He must also reduce his stock basis to zero.
B. He must recognize dividend income of $170,000 and reduce his stock basis to zero.
C. He must recognize dividend income of $200,000. His stock basis remains the same.
D. He must recognize dividend income of $150,000 and wage income of $20,000. He must also reduce his stock basis to zero.

41. What is the tax rate applicable to built-in gains for an S corporation?

A. 15%
B. 20%
C. 21%
D. 35%

42. When calculating the ordinary income of a partnership, which of the following is allowed as a deduction from ordinary income?

A. Delinquent federal taxes.
B. Short-term capital losses.
C. Guaranteed payments to partners.
D. Charitable contributions to exempt entities.

43. The Saluki Trust is a U.S. trust. The trust has a governing instrument that requires all income to be distributed in the current year. It is not a qualified disability trust. What is the Saluki Trust's exemption amount in 2021?

A. $100
B. $300
C. $600
D. $4,300

44. What will *increase* a shareholder's stock basis in an S corporation?

A. The shareholder's share of nondeductible expenses.
B. Additional paid-in capital to the corporation.
C. The shareholder's share of corporate and tax-exempt income.
D. Both B and C are correct.

45. In general, which of the following entities do not require any type of written document or state filings in order to be established?

A. A general partnership and a sole proprietorship.
B. An LLC and a sole proprietorship.
C. An S corporation and a sole proprietorship.
D. A general partnership or a limited liability partnership.

46. Kyle transfers a large tract of unimproved land to Alpine Investments, Inc. in exchange for stock. Immediately after the transfer, Kyle has majority control of the corporation and owns 85% of the outstanding stock. The remaining 15% is owned by another stockholder who is unrelated to Kyle. Alpine Investments, Inc. is a C corporation as well as an investment company. Is this a qualified section 351 exchange, or is the transfer a taxable event?

A. Yes, this is a qualified section 351 exchange. The exchange is not a taxable event.
B. No, it is not a qualified 351 exchange because Kyle does not own 90% of the outstanding stock.
C. No, it is not a qualified 351 exchange because Kyle does not own 100% of the outstanding stock.
D. No, it is not a qualified 351 exchange because Alpine Investments, Inc. is an investment company.

47. Distributions of stock dividends are generally tax-free to shareholders *except* when:

A. The distribution is made at the end of the corporation's fiscal year.
B. The distribution is only made to shareholders.
C. Some shareholders can receive cash or other property, and other shareholders receive stock.
D. The distribution is made by a foreign corporation or by a member of a controlled group of corporations.

48. An employer identification number (EIN) is for use _____.

A. In connection with business activities.
B. In place of a social security number.
C. In place of an ITIN.
D. For the identification of a foreign person.

49. Which of the following is a characteristic of a *complex* trust?

A. A trust that must distribute all of its income currently.
B. A trust that cannot make any distributions of principal.
C. A trust that is allowed to accumulate income.
D. A trust that has a $300 exemption.

50. Apple Valley Partnership has two general partners, Douglas and Craig, who share income and losses equally. Apple Valley had $110,000 of net ordinary income during the year. Craig received a cash distribution of $31,000 on September 12, 2021. Douglas received a cash distribution of $42,000 on May 1, 2021. Apple Valley is a cash-basis, calendar-year partnership. How much taxable income will Apple Valley report on Craig's Schedule K-1 and on Douglas's Schedule K-1?

A. Craig: $31,000; Douglas: $42,000
B. Craig: $55,000; Douglas: $55,000
C. Craig: $24,000; Douglas: $13,000
D. Craig: $79,000; Douglas: $68,000

51. Under the employer shared responsibility provisions of the Affordable Care Act, employers with at least 50 full-time employees (or full-time equivalent employees) are required to offer what type of insurance coverage?

A. Worker's compensation insurance.
B. Accident and health insurance.
C. Health insurance that provides minimum value.
D. Health, vision, and dental insurance that provides minimum value.

52. Zach is a sole proprietor whose business office was damaged by flooding. The adjusted basis of the assets damaged was $200,000, which included machinery and equipment that was completely destroyed in the flood. He received an insurance reimbursement of $140,000 and reinvested the entire amount plus $60,000 of additional funds to repair his damaged office and replace equipment. How should he report his casualty loss?

A. Report a loss of $60,000 on Form 4684.
B. Report a loss of $60,000 directly on Schedule C under "other expenses."
C. Report a loss of $60,000 on Schedule D.
D. Report a loss of $59,000 on Schedule A.

53. Kathryn and Fernand form Orchard Farms Partnership. Fernand contributes $100,000 of cash. Kathryn contributes farmland with an FMV of $90,000 and a tax basis of $10,000. Kathryn also contributes depreciable farming equipment that has an FMV of $50,000 and a tax basis of $75,000. Kathryn and Fernand each acquire a 50% interest in the partnership. What is Orchard Farms' tax basis in the equipment and the land?

Partnership's Tax Basis		
	Land	Equipment
A.	$90,000	$75,000
B.	$90,000	$50,000
C.	$10,000	$50,000
D.	$10,000	$75,000

54. Meritor Consulting, Inc. is a calendar-year, cash-basis C corporation. In 2021, Meritor Inc. has $100,000 of capital losses and $50,000 of capital gains. The corporation's capital gains for the <u>prior</u> three years are:

- 2018: $0 activity
- 2019: $24,000 capital gains
- 2020: $9,000 capital gains

Based on this information, what is Meritor, Inc.'s capital loss <u>carryforward</u> for 2022?

A. $16,000
B. $17,000
C. $24,000
D. $50,000

55. Form 3115 is used by a business to:

A. Report cash payments over $10,000.
B. Choose entity classification.
C. Report partnership income.
D. Apply for a change in accounting method.

56. Which of the following would NOT be section 1250 property?

A. A rental duplex.
B. A copyright.
C. A factory.
D. An office building.

57. Germana paid $30,000 to acquire a 30% stake in the Harvest Bagels, a general partnership she formed with two of her friends. Harvest Bagels is a calendar-year, cash-basis partnership. Germana is a general partner and her 30% stake allows her to share in capital and profits according to her ownership percentage. In its first year, Harvest Bagels earns ordinary income of $40,000. All of the profits were reinvested in the business, so no cash distributions are made to any of the partners during the year. How much income should Germana report on her return, and what is her partnership basis at the end of the year?

	Income	Germana's Year-End Basis
A.	$0	$42,000
B.	$10,000	$36,000
C.	$12,000	$42,000
D.	$0	$30,000

58. Aspen Ski Resort, Inc. is a cash-basis C corporation. During the year, Aspen Ski Resort distributed property with a fair market value of $260,000 and an adjusted basis of $40,000 to its sole shareholder, Misty. The property was subject to a $100,000 outstanding loan, which Misty personally assumed. This was not a liquidating distribution, and the corporation had applicable earnings and profits of $700,000. What is the amount of income that Misty would report from this transaction, and what is her basis in the property distributed?

A. Taxable dividend of $220,000; Misty's basis in the property is $260,000.
B. Taxable dividend of $220,000; Misty's basis in the property is $160,000.
C. Taxable dividend of $160,000; Misty's basis in the property is $260,000.
D. Misty does not have to report any taxable dividends. Her basis in the property is $220,000.

59. Kolby is a self-employed fitness trainer that visits and trains his clients in their homes. He drove 10,000 total miles in 2021, and 5,000 of those miles were for business purposes. Kolby's actual auto expenses were as follows:

- $100 replacement tire.
- $1,000 car insurance.
- $1,500 gasoline.
- $6,000 auto repairs.
- $500 oil changes.

Kolby decides to deduct actual costs, rather than use the standard mileage rate. Based on the above information, what is his *allowable* automobile expense on Schedule C?

A. $3,100
B. $4,550
C. $8,100
D. $9,100

60. Concord Candy, Inc. is a C Corporation. At the beginning of the year, Concord Candy, Inc. has $120,000 of accumulated earnings and profits. During the year, Concord Candy has current earnings of $90,000. On December 31, Concord Candy distributes $220,000 to Wendy, its sole shareholder. At the time of the distribution, Wendy's stock basis was zero. How does this distribution affect the corporation's earnings and profits, and how would Wendy report this distribution?

A. The distribution reduces Concord Candy's E&P to zero. Wendy must report dividend income of $210,000 and a capital gain of $10,000 on her Form 1040.
B. The distribution reduces Concord Candy's E&P to zero. Wendy must report dividend income of $220,000 on her Form 1040.
C. The distribution reduces Concord Candy's E&P to $120,000. Wendy must report ordinary income of $210,000 and a capital gain of $10,000 on her Form 1040.
D. The distribution reduces Concord Candy's E&P to $10,000. Wendy must report dividend income of $210,000 and a capital gain of $10,000 on her Form 1040.

61. Marsha is weighing her options as she decides on the best entity for her new business. Her primary concerns are raising capital from potential investors and avoiding personal liability. Without knowing other considerations, what entity structure might be most advantageous for Marsha?

A. Partnership.
B. S corporation.
C. C corporation.
D. Sole proprietorship.

62. Declan is a 50% shareholder in Red Rock Masonry, Inc., a calendar-year S corporation. His stock basis was $16,000 on January 1. At the end of the year, Red Rock Inc. had the following income and distributions:

Ordinary income	$80,000
Municipal bond interest income	$6,000
Year-end nondividend distribution to Declan	$50,000

What is Declan's stock basis in Red Rock Masonry at the end of the year *after* the nondividend distribution?

A. $9,000
B. $12,000
C. $30,000
D. $43,000

63. Which of the following is NOT subject to the net investment income tax (NIIT) on its investment income?

A. Individual.
B. C corporation.
C. Estate.
D. Trust.

64. Lathan, Tom, Jessica, and Shannon are all equal partners in the Paso Partnership. During the year, Paso Partnership borrows $100,000 for the construction of a storage facility for its products. All the partners are equally liable for the debt. Before borrowing the money, Lathan's partnership basis was $46,000. What effect does the construction loan have on Lathan's basis, if any?

A. Lathan's partnership basis is increased to $71,000.
B. Lathan's partnership basis is decreased to $21,000.
C. Lathan's partnership basis is increased to $146,000.
D. This transaction has no effect on the partnership's basis.

65. Nicholas is a 50% partner in the Lander Partnership. According to the partnership agreement, Nicholas is contracted to receive a $10,000 guaranteed payment every year. At the end of the year, after calculating all allowable deductions, Lander Partnership has net ordinary income of $42,000. Based on this information, how much partnership income will Nicholas report on his individual tax return for the year?

A. $10,000
B. $21,000
C. $31,000
D. $42,000

66. The Montague Disability Trust is a qualified disability trust (QDT), set up for the exclusive benefit of a disabled individual. What amount is the Montague Trust allowed as a personal exemption in 2021?

A. $0
B. $100
C. $300
D. $4,300

67. Which of the following is eligible to be a "disregarded entity" for federal tax purposes?

A. A corporation that is exempt from tax under Section 501(c)(3).
B. A corporation that elected S corporation status.
C. A single-member limited liability company (LLC).
D. A limited liability partnership (LLP).

68. Jonnie is a 30% partner in the Silver Partnership, which was newly formed in 2021. His starting basis in the partnership was $0. On December 31, 2021, Silver Partnership reports Jonnie's allocable share of ordinary income as $10,000. Jonnie also has an allocable share of $1,500 of municipal bond interest from the partnership. No cash distributions were made to Jonnie during the year. On January 15, 2022, a year in which the partnership did not have any income or expenses, it distributes $11,000 in cash to Jonnie. What is the effect of these transactions on Jonnie's partnership basis? How much taxable income must Jonnie report and in which year is the income taxable?

A. He must report $10,000 of taxable partnership income in 2021. After the distribution, his remaining partnership basis would be $500.
B. He must report $11,500 of taxable partnership income in 2022. After the distribution, his remaining partnership basis would be $500.
C. He must report $10,000 of taxable partnership income in 2022. After the distribution, his remaining partnership basis would be $1,000.
D. He must report $11,000 of taxable partnership income in 2022. After the distribution, his remaining partnership basis would be $0.

69. Theodore is a software programmer and computer repairman who reports his business income and loss on Schedule C. He creates a new software program for one of his clients, an auto dealership, to use at its business location. Theodore charges the dealership $24,000 for his program. Rather than paying the invoice with cash or a cash equivalent, the dealership gives Theodore a new minivan with an FMV of $24,500. Theodore agrees to accept the minivan in lieu of a cash payment. The dealership's cost basis in the minivan is $22,300. At the time he takes possession of the minivan, Theodore is required to pay sales tax totaling $960. Theodore plans to use the minivan exclusively for his business. Based on this information, what is Theodore's depreciable basis in the minivan?

A. $22,300
B. $24,000
C. $24,500
D. $24,960

70. Great Basin Corporation liquidated during the year by distributing assets with a fair market value of $200,000 to its five shareholders. The assets had an adjusted basis of $62,000. How would this transaction be treated for tax purposes by the corporation?

A. The distribution is not treated as a sale. Great Basin does not recognize gain or loss.
B. The distribution is treated as a sale. Great Basin recognizes a loss of $62,000.
C. The distribution is treated as a sale. Great Basin recognizes income of $200,000.
D. The distribution is treated as a sale. Great Basin recognizes income of $138,000.

71. Trevor is a self-employed electrician who files a Schedule C. In 2021, he drove his company van 7,000 business-related miles out of a total of 10,000 miles and had $5,500 in total gasoline expenses. He also had to pay $25 for the annual state license tags, $20 for an auto registration sticker, and $235 in DMV fees. The delivery van had been fully depreciated prior to the current year. He is claiming actual car expenses, rather than using the standard mileage rate. What amount can Trevor deduct on his Schedule C for automobile expenses?

A. $3,500
B. $4,046
C. $5,780
D. $8,137

72. Dillard Energy, Inc. is an S corporation. In 2021, Dillard Energy's S election was revoked, and the corporation reverted back to a C corporation. How long must Dillard Energy normally wait before electing S status again?

A. One year.
B. Two years.
C. Five years.
D. A corporation cannot elect S status again after it has been revoked.

73. Kistar Corporation owns 25% of the outstanding stock in Dover Corporation. Kistar and Dover are both C Corporations. In 2021, Dover Corporation issues a $10,000 dividend to Kistar Corporation. Ignoring any income limitations, what is Kistar Corporation's dividends-received deduction?

A. $0
B. $6,500
C. $8,000
D. $10,000

74. Connor died on April 10, 2021, leaving two minor children as his heirs. His estate was valued at $13 million on the date of his death, so an estate tax return must be filed. Which of the following expenses may be claimed as a deduction on the estate tax return?

A. Property taxes that accrued after the date of Connor's death.
B. Daycare expenses incurred after Connor's death on behalf of his surviving children.
C. Federal estate taxes paid.
D. Attorney's fees for work on behalf of Connor's estate.

75. Leggett Financial, Inc. acquired the following business assets during the year. Which of these assets is *not* eligible for Section 179 depreciation?

A. Trademark.
B. Business-use vehicle.
C. Used office furniture.
D. Off-the-shelf software.

76. Easton Auto Parts, Inc. is a calendar-year C corporation that was formally dissolved on July 12, 2021. When is the final tax return due for Easton Auto Parts?

A. April 18, 2022.
B. December 15, 2021.
C. October 17, 2022.
D. November 15, 2021.

77. Gabe has investments in several partnerships. In which of the following instances would Gabe be treated as having "constructive ownership" of *more* than 50% of the partnership?

Partnership Ownership Percentages
A. Gabe 20%; Gabe's son 20%; Gabe's brother 60%.
B. Gabe 25%; Gabe's wife 10%; Gabe's aunt 65%.
C. Gabe 45%; Gabe's step-brother 51%; Gabe's son 3%.
D. Gabe 45%; Gabe's cousin 55%.

78. Brett is the sole shareholder in Musset Corporation, a calendar-year S corporation. His stock basis is $24,000. Musset Corporation makes a nondividend distribution of $30,000 to Brett at the end of the year. How would the $6,000 distribution in excess of his stock basis be taxed?

A. He must report a capital gain of $6,000.
B. He must report an ordinary dividend of $6,000.
C. He must report a capital loss of $6,000.
D. He must reduce his stock basis to $6,000.

79. Which of the following retirement plans is allowed to offer loans to its participants?

A. SIMPLE-IRA.
B. Traditional IRA.
C. SIMPLE 401(k) plan.
D. SEP-IRA.

80. Tripp is a self-employed sheep farmer who files on Schedule F. On September 12, 2021, his farm was damaged and many of his livestock were killed by a hurricane. His farm was located in a Federally Declared Disaster Area. Tripp applied for disaster assistance and filed for insurance reimbursement to replace his livestock and repair his farm. He receives an insurance reimbursement on December 15, 2021, but he doesn't purchase replacement livestock right away. What is the replacement period for the sale or exchange of livestock in an area eligible for federal disaster assistance?

A. One year after the close of the first tax year in which the taxpayer realizes any part of his gain from the sale or exchange of livestock.
B. Two years after the close of the first tax year in which the taxpayer realizes any part of his gain from the sale or exchange of livestock.
C. Three years after the close of the first tax year in which the taxpayer realizes any part of his gain from the sale or exchange of livestock.
D. Four years after the close of the first tax year in which the taxpayer realizes any part of his gain from the sale or exchange of livestock.

81. Sunway Engineering, LLP is a calendar-year, cash-basis partnership. In 2021, Sunway Engineering provided industrial drafting services to a client, and in exchange the partnership received machinery with a fair market value of $8,000 and an adjusted basis of $7,500. The partnership also received website design services with a value of $3,000 from the same client. What amount must Sunway Engineering report as income from this transaction?

A. $0
B. $3,000
C. $10,500
D. $11,000

82. Schein Accountancy, LLP has two general partners that manage the day-to-day operations. Schein Accountancy also has two employees, a receptionist and a paid intern. Which of the following taxes would not be applicable to Schein Accountancy?

A. Federal income tax.
B. Excise taxes.
C. Federal unemployment (FUTA) tax.
D. Social Security and Medicare taxes (for employees' wages).

83. All of the following business expenses are deductible on Schedule C except _____.

A. Long-distance telephone expenses.
B. Interest paid on business loans.
C. Legal and professional services and fees.
D. Health insurance premiums for a self-employed taxpayer.

84. Which of the following exchanges could be a qualified like-kind exchange of property under IRC section 1031?

A. An exchange of a rental condo in New York with a rental condo in Cancun, Mexico.
B. An exchange of an undeveloped lot for a factory building.
C. An exchange of a primary residence for a rental duplex.
D. An exchange of one type of cryptocurrency for a different cryptocurrency.

85. Hesperia Health, Inc. offers many types of fringe benefits to its employees. Which of the following benefits would not be deductible by the corporation in 2021?

A. Health insurance provided to an employee.
B. Term-life insurance coverage provided to an employee.
C. Employer-provided transit passes.
D. Educational assistance program.

86. Culver Packard Inc., an accrual-basis C corporation, owes one of its vendors $250,000 for a delinquent invoice from the prior tax year. The vendor threatens to sue to recover the debt. Culver Packard Inc. agrees to transfer a commercial building to the vendor in order to satisfy the debt. Culver Packard Inc.'s basis in the building is $190,000. How must this transaction be reported?

A. The corporation recognizes a taxable gain of $60,000.
B. The corporation recognizes forgiven debt income of $190,000.
C. The corporation recognizes a taxable gain of $250,000.
D. The corporation recognizes a loss of $60,000.

87. An activity is presumed to be engaged in for profit, rather than a hobby, if:

A. The activity shows a profit for two out of the last five years, including the current year.
B. The activity shows a profit for two out of the last seven years, *not* including the current year.
C. The activity shows a profit for three out of the last five years, *not* including the current year.
D. The activity shows a profit for three out of the last five years, including the current year.

88. A city charges a fee for installing sidewalk curbing in front of a business. This is a type of:

A. Repair that can be deducted as a current expense.
B. Assessment that is added to the property's basis.
C. Real estate tax that can be deducted as a current expense.
D. Nondeductible tax.

89. Sadie owns a retail shop. She recently signed a contract with a vendor, which was finalized over dinner. The total cost of the meal was $250. Sadie's own dinner was $50. The vendor ate an expensive meal and also ordered dessert, so his portion of the meal was $170. The remainder of the bill was for the tip and tax. Sadie also spent $10 for a taxi ride to the dinner. How much of the evening's expense is deductible by Sadie as a business expense?

A. $60
B. $130
C. $140
D. $260

90. Warren died on October 18, 2021, leaving an estate valued at $33 million. His executor elects a calendar year for the estate. When is Form 1041 (the income tax return for the estate) due?

A. December 31, 2021.
B. March 15, 2022.
C. April 18, 2022.
D. September 18, 2022.

91. Keller is a professional artist who sells his artwork at regional fairs. He does not accept credit or debit cards. A customer buys five of Keller's paintings at a show, paying $12,500 in cash. What, if anything, is Keller's reporting responsibility for this type of payment?

A. He must report the income on Schedule C. He has no additional reporting requirement.
B. He must file Form 926.
C. He must file Form 1099-NEC.
D. He must report the income on Schedule C, as well as file Form 8300.

92. When using taxable income as a starting point, which of the following transactions *decreases* the amount of a C corporation's earnings and profits?

A. Long-term contracts reported on the completed contract method.
B. Mine exploration and development costs deducted currently.
C. Dividends-received deduction.
D. Corporate dividends and other distributions to shareholders.

93. Fruitman Cannery, Inc. purchases manufacturing equipment to use in its canning operations on August 1, 2021. The cost of the equipment is $250,000, not including $18,500 of additional sales tax. The entire purchase of the machinery is financed with a small business loan. During the year, Fruitman Cannery pays interest of $10,500 on the loan. What is the proper treatment of this transaction?

A. Fruitman Cannery must capitalize $279,000 as the total cost of the machine and record depreciation expense each year.
B. Fruitman Cannery can deduct the interest paid on the loan ($10,500). The other costs, including sales tax, should be capitalized and depreciated.
C. Fruitman Cannery can deduct all the costs, including the machine purchase, as a current business expense.
D. Fruitman Cannery can deduct the sales tax and the loan interest as business expenses.

94. Deborah is a general partner in the Deal-Wise Partnership. The adjusted basis of her partnership interest is $165,000. During the year, she receives a cash distribution of $80,000 and machinery with an adjusted basis of $28,000 and a fair market value of $30,000. This is a nonliquidating distribution. What is the basis of Deborah's partnership interest after these distributions?

A. $55,000
B. $57,000
C. $85,000
D. $113,000

95. Tri-Star Electronics, Inc. is a new C corporation with two equal shareholders, Kayla and Jamar. The corporation reports income and loss on a calendar-year basis. Kayla's stock basis at the beginning of the year is $50,000. Tri-Star Electronics has no accumulated earnings and profits at the beginning of the year, and has $64,000 of current earnings and profits. The corporation allocates its profits based on stock ownership. On December 31, Tri-Star Electronics distributes $40,000 to each shareholder. How much gain (or loss) must Kayla recognize on this distribution, and what is her ending stock basis?

	Income	Ending stock basis
A.	$40,000 dividend	$10,000
B.	$32,000 dividend	$10,000
C.	$40,000 dividend	$50,000
D.	$32,000 dividend	$42,000

96. Melanie is a self-employed architect. She generally travels to three different clients' offices each work day. It is 10 miles from her home to the first office and 5 miles from the last office back home. It is 13 miles from the first office to the second office and 5 miles from the second office to the third office. Melanie does not have a qualified home office. Melanie drives a total of 33 miles each workday. How many of these miles are deductible?

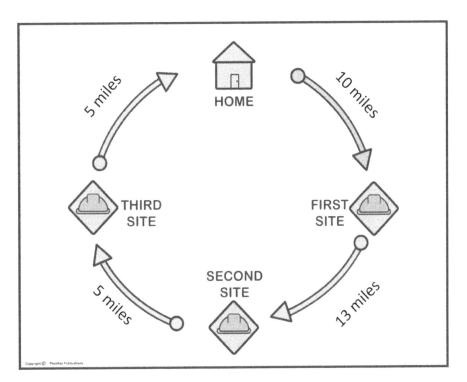

A. 10 miles per day.
B. 18 miles per day.
C. 23 miles per day.
D. 33 miles per day.

97. The Cascade Partnership is formed by the following partners, two of which are corporate partners and one of whom is an individual. None of the partners are related persons or related entities.

Partner	Ownership stake	Tax year-end
Daisy Corporation (C corp.)	10%	April 30
Maxim Corporation (C corp.)	45%	April 30
Elroy Smith (an individual)	45%	December 31

What is the required tax year-end for Cascade Partnership?

A. Cascade Partnership is allowed to select any tax year-end it chooses.
B. Cascade Partnership is required to use a calendar year-end.
C. Cascade Partnership is required to use April 30 as its tax year-end.
D. Cascade Partnership is required to use August 31 as its tax year-end.

98. Which of the following best describes a controlled group?

A. A privately held corporation that does not publicly list its financial statements.
B. A type of partnership controlled by fewer than five individuals.
C. A corporation or partnership that is owned by family members.
D. A group of corporations that are related through common ownership and are subject to rules regarding related party transactions.

99. Pioneer Shoes, Inc. is a shoe manufacturing company that had the following costs during the tax year:

Raw materials purchased	$5,400,000
Freight-in charges on raw materials purchased	$175,000
Manufacturing wages and benefits	$4,025,000
Selling and administrative wages and benefits	$500,000
Charitable contributions	$45,000
Other direct manufacturing costs	$875,000
Administrative office expense	$20,000
Costs of shipping finished products to customers	$150,000

Pioneer's inventory (including raw materials, work-in-process, and finished products) was $1,200,000 on January 1, 2021, and $1,575,000 on December 31, 2021. Based on these figures, what was the company's cost of goods sold for the year?

A. $10,100,000
B. $10,250,000
C. $10,815,000
D. $10,850,000

100. Tenant Industries, Inc. is a C corporation with 50 employees. In addition to Social Security and Medicare tax, what other type of employment tax would Tenant Industries be required to pay on the wages it pays to its employees?

A. Additional Medicare tax.
B. Federal income tax.
C. Accumulated earnings tax.
D. Federal unemployment tax.

Please review your answer choices with the correct answers in the next section.

Answers to Exam #1: Businesses

1. The answer is B. Brielle's allowable business deductions on Schedule C total **$3,847**. The standard mileage rate in 2021 is 56¢ per mile, so driving expenses are equal to 56 cents x 1,200 = $672. The total amount of allowable business expenses is calculated as follows: ($3,175 + $672 = **$3,847**). The self-employed health insurance would not be deductible on Schedule C. Instead, it would be an adjustment to income on Schedule 1 of her individual Form 1040.

2. The answer is D. A decedent's estate generally continues to exist until the final distribution of the estate's assets is made to the heirs and other beneficiaries. A decedent's estate is a taxable entity, considered *separate* from the decedent. An estate comes into existence at the time of the decedent's death (see the Instructions for Form 56, *Notice Concerning Fiduciary Relationship,* for more information).

3. The answer is C. Since the insurance policy that Elsewise Partnership purchased in advance is a *three-year* policy, the business must figure out the deductible portion that applies to the current year and capitalize the rest and deduct the remaining expense in the year to which it applies. If a cash-basis business pays an insurance premium in advance, it can generally deduct only the portion that applies to the current tax year, regardless of whether it prepaid the entire amount. Therefore, Elsewise Partnership may only deduct the part of the policy that applies to the current year, calculated as follows: $1,800 ÷ 36 (months) = $50 per month; $50 × 12 = **$600,** the current year insurance expense.

Note: While not applicable in this case, there is an exception under the "12-month rule," in which the amounts paid do not relate to periods beyond the earlier of:

- 12 months after the first date on which the business receives the benefit; or
- The end of the tax year following the tax year in which payment is made.

Under this exception, the payment can be deducted in full in the year paid, even though part of the period covered under the expense goes beyond the year of payment.

4. The answer is B. In general, a partner's basis in distributed property is the same as the partnership's basis in the property immediately before the distribution. However, in this case, the distributed property had a basis that exceeded Jiro's remaining basis in his partnership interest (after the reduction in his basis in the partnership by the $15,000 cash portion of the distribution). A partner's basis in distributed property cannot exceed his basis in the partnership. Therefore, Jiro's partnership basis is reduced to zero, and his basis in the land becomes $50,000.

Jiro's starting basis	$65,000
Cash distribution	15,000
Jiro's remaining basis after cash distribution	**$50,000**

5. The answer is A. An unincorporated business jointly owned by a married couple is generally classified as a partnership for federal tax purposes. However, a married couple who operate a business together may choose to file as a Qualified Joint Venture (QJV), filing on two separate Schedules C, and two Schedules SE, as long as they file jointly. Unless a business meets the requirements of a qualified joint venture, which includes that both spouses must materially participate in the business, a sole proprietorship must be solely owned by one spouse, although the other spouse may work in the business as an employee.

6. The answer is C. Form 1041, *U.S. Income Tax Return for Estates and Trusts*, is also used to report any income a trust earns over $600. Since the Perdue Trust has over $600 in gross income for the year, the trust must file a tax return. The fact that all the income went to charity and/or a political group is irrelevant to the trust's filing requirement; a Form 1041 still needs to be filed.

7. The answer is D. There is no "gross receipts" threshold for whether an entity must be taxed as a corporation. The following businesses formed after 1996 are automatically taxed as corporations:

- A business formed under a federal or state law that refers to it as a corporation.
- A business formed under a state law that refers to it as a joint-stock company or joint-stock association.
- Insurance companies and certain banks.
- A business owned by a state or local government.
- A business specifically required to be taxed as a corporation by the IRC (for example, certain publicly traded partnerships).
- Certain foreign businesses.
- Any other business that elects to be taxed as a corporation and files Form 8832, *Entity Classification Election.*

8. The answer is B. Cheryl has a $20,000 taxable dividend and a $10,000 capital gain. A distribution is treated as a dividend to the extent that the corporation has earnings and profits. The amount distributed to Cheryl would come first from the corporation's earnings and profits ($20,000) and be classified as a dividend. The remaining amount ($30,000 - $20,000) would be classified as a capital gain, because it exceeds Cheryl's stock basis, which is zero.

9. The answer is D. All of the above scenarios would trigger a filing requirement for a domestic trust. The fiduciary must file Form 1041 for a domestic trust (taxable under section 641) that has:

- Any *taxable* income for the tax year,
- Gross income of $600 or more (regardless of whether the income is taxable or not), or
- A beneficiary who is a nonresident alien.

10. The answer is D. Broadpoint, Inc.'s *taxable* income is determined as follows:

Net income per books	$300,000
Plus, federal income tax expense per books	$4,000
Plus, excess of capital losses over capital gains	$10,000
Minus the tax-exempt interest income	($5,000)
Taxable income	**$309,000**

Capital losses are only deductible up to the amount of capital gains for a C Corporation, so the *excess* of capital losses over capital gains must be added back in to calculate taxable income.

11. The answer is C. Fiscal-year estates and trusts must file Form 1041 by the 15th day of the 4th month following the close of the entity's tax year. In this example, the trust has a tax year that ends on May 30, so the trustee must file Form 1041 by **September 15.**

12. The answer is C. The "test rate" to determine if the loan is a below-market loan is the long-term applicable Federal rate as of the day the loan is made. If the loan is deemed to be a "below-market" loan, then the corporation must calculate imputed interest on the loan. The rules for below-market loans apply to:
- Gift loans
- Compensation-related loans
- Corporation-shareholder loans
- Tax avoidance loans, and
- Other below market loans.

(This question is modified from a released EA exam question. For more information on below-market loans, see IRS Publication 535 and Publication 550).

13. The answer is B. Fancy Flowers can deduct the cost as an advertising expense. Cash payments to a charitable organization may be deductible as business expenses if the payments *aren't* charitable contributions. In this case, Fancy Flowers was paying for advertising, so the cost would simply be a business expense on the partnership tax return. If a partnership *does* make a charitable contribution, the amount is reported on Schedule K-1, and each partner takes a percentage share of the deduction on his or her personal tax return. (See a similar example in IRS Publication 535, *Business Expenses*).

14. The answer is C. An S corporation cannot deduct charitable contributions. Only a C corporation can take a business deduction for charitable contributions. Charitable contributions made by an S corporation flow-through to the shareholders who may be able to deduct their share of the contributions on their own return (typically on Schedule A). The two main reasons for electing S corporation status are:
- Avoiding double taxation on distributions.
- Allowing corporate losses to pass through to shareholders.

Answer "D" is incorrect because S corporations share the same liability protection of C corporations.

15. The answer is D. A closely-held corporation generally has a small number of shareholders and no public market for its corporate stock. Corporate ownership and management often overlap. A corporation is considered to be "closely held" if all of the following apply:
- It is not a personal service corporation.
- At any time during the last half of the tax year, more than 50% of the value of its outstanding stock is, directly or indirectly, owned by five or fewer individuals. An individual, in this case, includes certain trusts and private foundations.

Closely held corporations are exempt from certain at-risk and passive activity loss limitation limits, which can provide substantial tax benefits.

16. The answer is A. Elaine may deduct Devin's wages as a business expense. Her son's wages are not subject to Social Security and Medicare taxes. Wages of a child under the age of 18 who works for a parent in a business are not subject to Social Security and Medicare taxes if the trade or business is a sole proprietorship, LLC or a partnership in which each partner is a parent of the child (this rule does not apply to corporations). Earned income, including wages that are paid to the taxpayer's own children, is not subject to the Kiddie tax, regardless of the child's age.

17. The answer is C. Sales taxes are *excluded* from gross receipts and deductible expenses. In states where sales tax is imposed on the *buyer*, the sales taxes collected by the seller are a liability, not income, and are therefore excluded from a business' gross receipts and deductible expenses, as the taxes are merely collected on behalf of the state. Note that in certain states, sales taxes are imposed on the *seller*, and in these states, a seller who collects sales tax from their customers must include the sales taxes in gross receipts and then deduct them when paid (or incurred).

> **Note:** When a business *pays* sales tax in connection with the purchase of goods or services, the tax is considered a component of the cost of the item purchased. Thus, if the item is depreciable property, the sales tax is added to its depreciable basis. If the item is merchandise for resale or to be used in the production of inventory, the tax is capitalized as a component of inventory.

18. The answer is C. Sherry will not be required to request an EIN if she operates multiple businesses, as long as those businesses are all sole proprietorships without employees. A taxpayer will need an EIN if any of the following is true:

- She files for bankruptcy under Chapter 7 (liquidation) or Chapter 11 (reorganization) of the Bankruptcy Code.
- She incorporates or takes in partners to operate as a partnership.
- She establishes a pension, profit-sharing, or retirement plan.
- She files employment or excise tax returns.
- She will not need a new EIN if any of the following is true:
- She changes the name of her business.
- She changes the location or adds locations (stores or branches of the same entity).
- She operates multiple businesses (including stores or branches of the same entity).

19. The answer is A. Estyle Aesthetics, Inc. is not entitled to a QBI deduction because it is a C corporation. C corporations can neither claim a section 199A deduction nor can their shareholders claim any 199A deduction from any income attributable to the corporation. Despite the fact that he is an owner, Lance is also not entitled to a section 199A deduction from this business. The section 199A deduction is *only* available to the owner(s) of the following businesses:

- Individual owners of sole proprietorships, rental properties, S corporations, or partnerships, and
- Trusts and estates that own an interest in the businesses listed above.

> **Note:** Income earned in a C corporation is not eligible for the section 199A deduction. The deduction is only available to individual and estate/trust owners of pass-through entities and sole proprietorships.

20. The answer is B. Gabby has a taxable gain of **$19,000**. Since only one-half of the duplex was a rental property, the gain and loss for the two portions of the building must be determined separately, as outlined in the following table. Gabby will have a taxable gain on the business portion of the property. The loss on the residential portion (where she lives) is not deductible.

Activity	Residential Part	Rental Part
Condemnation award received	$45,000	$45,000
Minus the legal fees	(1,000)	(1,000)
Net condemnation award	44,000	44,000
Adjusted basis calculation		
Original cost: $75,000 x 50%	37,500	37,500
Improvements: $15,000 x 50%	7,500	7,500
Total	45,000	45,000
Minus depreciation	N/A	(20,000)
Adjusted basis, business part	45,000	25,000
Loss/gain on property	**($1,000)**	**$19,000**

Since this was a condemnation, Gabby could elect to defer all the gain by reinvesting the condemnation award in a similar property, under the rules for involuntary conversions (IRC Section 1033).

21. The answer is B. Since Dominion Services, Inc. is on the accrual basis, it reports income when it is *earned*, not when it is received. The company must include the entire $22,000 in 2021 income because that is when it was *earned*.

22. The answer is C. Dunne Corp. can carry over any unused charitable contributions for five years. A C corporation can carry over charitable contributions for five years. It loses any unused amounts after that period. Corporate charitable contributions cannot be carried back.

> **Note:** In prior years, the annual charitable deduction by a corporation was generally limited to 10% of taxable income, while a 15% limit applied to charitable contributions of food inventory. Due to changes implemented by the CARES Act, corporations can claim a charitable income tax deduction of up to 25% of the corporation's taxable income in 2021. The 25% limit applies to cash donations as well as donations of food inventory to charitable organizations. Donations in excess of 25% may be carried over and deducted in the following five years. Donations of other property are still subject to the 10% limit.

23. The answer is B. Riaan recognizes a taxable gain of **$175,000** on the transaction. In order for the transfer to be nontaxable, Riaan would have to own at least 80% of the total stock. Since he only owned 70% of the stock after the transaction, the exchange does not qualify for section 351 nonrecognition treatment.

24. The answer is D. A business does not need to apply for a new EIN in any of the following instances:
- To change the name of a business.
- To change the location or add locations (stores, plants, enterprises, or branches of the same entity).
- If a sole proprietor operates multiple businesses (including stores, plants, enterprises, or branches of the same entity).

25. The answer is B. A revocable grantor trust generally does not require a tax return filing (Form 1041) as long as the grantor is still alive and/or not incapacitated. This is because the grantor maintains ownership of the assets. The income earned by a revocable grantor trust is generally reported on the grantor's individual Form 1040, not on a separate trust tax return. In general, most irrevocable trusts (including a qualified disability trust) must file an IRS Form 1041. Charitable trusts that are formed as private foundations must file Form 990-PF annually.

26. The answer is B. A corporation is always required to file a tax return, regardless of the level of activity. The filing requirement begins when the corporation is created, and continues until the entity is dissolved. Answer "C" is incorrect, because a partnership is not required to file a return unless it neither receives income nor incurs any expenditures treated as deductions or credits for federal income tax purposes. Answer "A" is incorrect because not all exempt entities are required to file a return, based on their gross income and the type of activities that they engage in (for example, churches and religious organizations are not required to file an annual information return). Answer "D" is incorrect because, in general, only estates with a specified amount of gross income are required to file income tax returns.

27. The answer is D. An individual partner's basis is increased by his share of taxable and nontaxable income. Since Christian is a 50% partner, the income items must be allocated based on his partnership percentage. The answer is calculated as follows:

Calculations for Copperleaf Partnership	Partnership Income	Christian's Portion
Starting partnership basis		$1,000
Ordinary income x 50%	$40,000	$20,000
Tax-exempt income x 50%	$20,000	$10,000
Rental income x 50%	$4,000	$2,000
Christian's year-end partnership basis		**$33,000**

28. The answer is A. A business can set up a SIMPLE IRA plan effective on any date between January 1 and October 1, (provided the business did not previously maintain another SIMPLE IRA plan). A *later* effective date is allowed only when the business is started after October 1. For example, a company that begins operations for the first time in November can establish a SIMPLE IRA in November.

29. The answer is D. Section 1245 applies to most depreciable personal property, but generally does not apply to real property (buildings, factories, farmland, residential rental properties, etc.). Section 1245 property does not include most permanent buildings and structural components. The term "building" also includes a house, barn, warehouse, or garage. However, there is an exception in the law for certain "single purpose" agricultural and storage structures. This would include something like a greenhouse, oil and gas storage structures, a piggery, stable, or a grain silo.

30. The answer is B. For tax year 2021, the standard mileage rate is 56¢ per mile. Based on the question, Roger incurred 6,800 business miles x 56¢ standard mileage rate = **$3,808** mileage deduction.

31. The answer is C. An S corporation is a pass-through entity. Partnerships and S corporations are pass-through entities and are generally not taxed on their earnings.

32. The answer is C. Treeland Nursery's *total* gain on the sale is $94,000 ($180,000 - $86,000). Because the greenhouse is section 1245 property, Treeland Nursery must recognize **$39,000** of ordinary income from depreciation recapture. The remaining **$55,000** is capital gain from the sale of a section 1231 asset.

33. The answer is D. Bruce's basis is **$5,875.** All the costs must be added to the machine's basis ($5,500 + $125 + $250) = $5,875. An asset's basis includes shipping fees and installation costs (basically, costs incurred to make the asset ready for its initial use).

34. The answer is B. Partnerships and C corporations cannot own stock in an S corporation. Estates, certain trusts, individuals, and some exempt entities (specifically, 501(c)(3) entities) are permitted to own stock in an S corporation. An S corporation can have up to 100 shareholders, and it can have both voting and nonvoting stock, as long as there is only one class of stock.

35. The answer is A. The accumulated earnings tax is a 20% tax assessed on the excess accumulated earnings and profits of a C corporation. If a corporation allows earnings to accumulate beyond the reasonable needs of the business, it may be subject to an accumulated earnings tax of 20% of the excess amount accumulated. The accumulated earnings tax does not apply to partnerships, sole proprietorships, or S corporations, because these businesses are pass-through entities and do not accumulate earnings from year to year as a C corporation does. For most C corporations, there is a $250,000 minimum credit against this tax ($150,000 for corporations providing professional services).

36. The answer is D. Montana Equine Rescue must file Form 990 by May 15. The organization may also request an extension by using Form 8868. Even though a charity may be organized as a corporation, it must still file Form 990, not Form 1120. An exempt entity is required to file by the fifteenth of the fifth month after the end of its taxable year. For calendar-year exempt entities, their return is due May 15. The extended due date is generally November 15 (6 months after the normal due date).

37. The answer is A. The excessive part of Colson's salary will be treated as a constructive distribution. If a corporation pays an employee who is also a shareholder a salary that is treated unreasonably high considering the services actually performed, the excessive part of the salary may be reclassified as a constructive distribution of earnings to the employee-shareholder. The distribution is treated as a dividend, which means it is taxable to the shareholder, but not deductible by the C corporation. Therefore, constructive distributions (also called "constructive dividends") have a very negative impact on the corporation.

38. The answer is B. Kerry's basis in her partnership interest is calculated by adding the cash she contributed ($10,000) to the basis of the property she contributed ($18,000). Her partnership interest is **$28,000** ($10,000 + $18,000).

39. The answer is C. An S corporation's accumulated adjustment account includes all items of income and expenses with the *exception* of tax-exempt income (and any expenses related to tax-exempt income).

40. The answer is A. Christopher must recognize dividend income of $150,000 and a taxable capital gain of $20,000. He must also reduce his stock basis to zero. In this case, the shareholder received dividend income of $150,000 (equal to the corporation's accumulated earnings and profits). Christopher's stock basis was $30,000, so, after reducing his stock basis to zero (for the tax-free return of capital for the $30,000 of distributions following the $150,000 of taxable dividends), he must recognize a taxable gain of $20,000, which is the excess of the distribution over the amount of his stock basis. The answer is calculated as follows:

($200,000 distribution - $150,000 accumulated E&P) = $50,000
$50,000 remaining distribution - $30,000 return of capital
(Stock basis reduced to zero) = $20,000
$20,000 is treated as a capital gain from the sale or exchange of stock.

41. The answer is C. The built-in gains tax (also called the "BIG tax") is imposed at the highest rate of tax that is applicable to corporations. This tax only potentially applies to S corporations which were previously C corporations, and later converted (or when an S corporation acquires a C Corporation). Corporate tax rates are set at a flat tax rate of 21%, so the built-in gains tax rate is also 21%.

42. The answer is C. Guaranteed payments are paid in accordance with the partnership agreement, and they are treated like salary payments to employees. Guaranteed payments are deductible in determining the partnership's ordinary income. The amounts are specifically allocated to the individual partners who received guaranteed payments on their Schedule K-1, which are then taxed as self-employment income on the partner's individual return, in addition to being subject to income tax.

43. The answer is B. A trust whose governing instrument requires that all income be distributed currently (i.e., a "simple trust") is allowed a $300 exemption, even if it distributed amounts other than income during the tax year. For more information, see the IRS instructions for Form 1041, *U.S. Income Tax Return for Estates and Trusts.*

Note: Although personal exemptions are currently suspended for *individuals*, trusts and estates are still allowed a personal exemption under IRC section 642(b).

44. The answer is D. A shareholder's basis in an S corporation will increase with:

- Additional contributions to capital, and
- The shareholder's share of corporate and tax-exempt income.

Note: When PPP loan forgiveness is granted, the amounts are treated as tax-exempt income for partnership and S corporation basis purposes. Therefore, the adjusted basis of a shareholder's stock in an S corporation will be increased by the tax-free income resulting from the forgiveness of PPP loans. Rev. Proc. 2021-48 provides guidance on the appropriate timing of receipt of PPP forgiveness tax-exempt income.

45. The answer is A. Neither a general partnership nor a sole proprietorship requires any type of formal agreement or state filing in order to be created. A corporation, limited partnership (LLP, LP, or LLLP) and an LLC (limited liability company) each requires formal filing at the state level in order for the entity to be created.

46. The answer is D. The transfer is not a qualified 351 exchange because Alpine Investments, Inc. is an investment company. In an eligible section 351 exchange, no gain or loss is recognized provided:

- The transferor receives only stock in exchange for property (or money), and
- The transferor is in control of the corporation immediately after the transfer. This means at least 80% of the voting stock and at least 80% of all other classes of stock of the corporation.

However, section 351 does not apply when:

- The corporation is an investment company.
- The transferor transfers property during a bankruptcy in exchange for stock used to pay creditors.

The stock received in exchange for the corporation's debt (other than a security) or for interest on the corporation's debt (including a security) that accrued while the transferor held the debt.

47. The answer is C. A distribution that gives cash or other property to some shareholders, and an increase in the percentage interest in the corporation's assets or earnings and profits to other shareholders, would cause a stock dividend to be a taxable event. Generally, stock dividends and stock rights are not taxable. However, in the following cases, a stock dividend would be taxable:

- The distribution gives cash or other property to some shareholders, and an increase in the percentage interest in the corporation's assets or earnings and profits to other shareholders.
- Shareholders are permitted to choose cash or other property instead of stock or stock rights.
- The distribution is in convertible preferred stock, or some shareholders receive preferred stock and others receive common stock.

If a stock dividend is deemed taxable, it would be included in the shareholder's income at its FMV at the time of distribution.

48. The answer is A. An EIN is generally for use in connection with business activities. A taxpayer should not use an EIN in place of a social security number (SSN) or individual taxpayer identification number (ITIN).

49. The answer is C. A *complex* trust may accumulate income. A simple trust may not. Any trust that is not a simple trust is automatically a complex trust. Complex trusts may accumulate income, distribute amounts other than current income and make charitable gifts. A simple trust must distribute all its income currently. A simple trust cannot accumulate income, distribute principal, or pay money for charitable purposes.

50. The answer is B. Douglas and Craig share income and loss equally, and they are required to report their share of partnership income, regardless of whether it is distributed. Therefore, each partner will report **$55,000** ($110,000 × 50%) of taxable income from the partnership. An individual partner must report his "allocable share" of partnership income on his own tax return (Form 1040, Schedule E). The partner's allocable share of partnership income is reported to each individual partner on Schedule K-1.

51. The answer is C. Under the employer shared responsibility provisions of the Affordable Care Act, employers with at least 50 full-time employees (or full-time equivalent employees) are required to offer health insurance that provides minimum value, or "minimum essential coverage." Employers are not required to provide vision or dental coverage. Employers with fewer than 50 full-time or full-time equivalent employees are not subject to these provisions.

52. The answer is A. Zach should report a loss of **$60,000** on Form 4684. Deductible losses related to business and income-producing property are reported on Form 4684, *Casualties and Thefts*, and on Form 4797, *Sales of Business Property*. Losses from a business casualty are fully deductible. His loss deduction is reduced by the amount of his insurance reimbursement.

53. The answer is D. Generally, the partnership's basis in any contributed property is identical to the adjusted basis of the property in the hands of the contributing partner. Therefore, the partnership's tax basis in the contributed land is **$10,000** (the same basis that Kathryn had in the land). The partnership's tax basis in the contributed equipment is **$75,000**. In addition, the partnership's holding period for the assets is the same as Kathryn's holding period, so if either asset is later sold, the partner's holding period is "tacked on" for purposes of determining the partnership's recognition of long-term or short-term gain or loss.

54. The answer is B. Meritor, Inc.'s capital loss carryforward for 2022 is **$17,000**. As stated in the question, the net capital losses for 2021 are $50,000 ($100,000 - $50,000). Corporate net capital losses are carried back three years and carried forward five years. The net capital losses cannot be carried back to 2018 because there were no capital gains that year, so the $24,000 in gains from 2019 must be offset first. This leaves $26,000 of capital losses. The $9,000 of capital gains from 2020 may also be offset, which leaves a carryforward of $17,000. This carryforward may be applied to any capital gains that are earned in the subsequent five tax years.

> **Note:** Unlike individual taxpayers, a C corporation's capital losses may not offset a corporation's ordinary income; capital losses may **only** offset capital gains.

55. The answer is D. A taxpayer must file Form 3115, *Application for Change in Accounting Method*, to request a change in either an overall accounting method or the accounting treatment for an individual item. No user fee is required.

56. The answer is B. A copyright is intangible personal property, and is section 1245 property, not section 1250 property. Examples of intangible personal property include: patents, franchise rights, copyrights, and trademarks. Section 1250 property generally consists of buildings (including their structural components), other inherently permanent structures, and land improvements of general use and purpose. Examples of section 1250 property include: residential rental property, factory buildings, and office buildings.

57. The answer is C. Even though no distributions were made during the year, Germana is required to report her share of the partnership's income. The income is allocated based on her partnership interest, so the answer is calculated as follows: (30% × $40,000 partnership income) = **$12,000** of ordinary income to Germana, which increases her partnership basis. Since no distributions were made, her year-end basis is as follows: ($30,000 starting basis + $12,000 income) = **$42,000.**

58. The answer is C. Misty must report a taxable dividend of **$160,000** ($260,000 FMV - $100,000 liability assumed). Her basis in the property is **$260,000**. When a corporation distributes property to a shareholder (rather than stock or cash), the amount distributed is based on the FMV of the property on the date of distribution. The amount distributed is reduced by any liabilities assumed by the shareholder. The basis of the property in the hands of the shareholder would be the FMV on the date of distribution.

59. The answer is B. Kolby's total automobile expenses are $9,100 ($100 + $1,000 + $1,500 + $6,000 + $500). Since Kolby used the car for business purposes only 50% of the time, (5,000 business miles ÷ 10,000 total miles), his *allowable* deduction for auto expenses is **$4,550** ($9,100 x 50% = $4,550). If we use the same figures to calculate Kolby's deduction using the standard mileage rate, Kolby can multiply his business mileage by the standard mileage rate (56 cents per mile in 2021 X 5,000 miles), which would equal a deduction of $2,800. So, in this case, Kolby would get a larger deduction taking "actual costs" instead of the standard mileage rate. In this example, the taxpayer is able to deduct more by using the "Actual Expenses" method than by using the Standard Mileage method. He also would be allowed to claim depreciation on his vehicle, in addition to the deductible expenses above.

60. The answer is A. The distribution reduces Concord Candy's E&P to zero. Wendy must report dividend income of $210,000 and a capital gain of $10,000. The answer is calculated as follows:

Accumulated E&P	$120,000
Current year E&P	90,000
Current and accumulated E&P	**$210,000**

A distribution cannot create a deficit in a corporation's earnings and profits. Thus, the distribution to Wendy reduces E&P to zero.

Gross distribution	$220,000
Subtract current and accumulated E&P	210,000
Capital gain to Wendy	**$10,000**

Wendy must recognize a dividend of $210,000 (the amount of the distribution from current and accumulated E&P), and the remaining $10,000 would either reduce her stock basis or produce a capital gain for her. Since the question stated that Wendy's stock basis was already zero, the $10,000 would be reported as a capital gain.

61. The answer is C. Marsha should consider forming a C Corporation. One of the main advantages of a corporation is limited liability for directors, officers, shareholders, and employees. When forming a corporation, prospective shareholders provide money, property, or both in exchange for the issuance of the corporation's capital stock. A corporation is considered an entity separate from its shareholders and must elect a board of directors who are responsible for oversight of the company. In choosing between an S corporation and a C corporation, the latter structure will generally provide more options for raising capital since it will not be subject to restrictions on the number and types of shareholders that apply to S corporations.

62. The answer is A. The answer is calculated as follows:

Declan's starting basis	$16,000
Ordinary income (× 50%)	$40,000
Exempt income (× 50%)	$3,000
Year-end basis (before distribution)	**$59,000**
Subtract distribution	($50,000)
Year-end basis (after distribution)	**$9,000**

63. The answer is B. The net investment income tax (NIIT) does not apply to C corporations. The NIIT applies at a rate of 3.8% to certain investment income of individuals, estates and trusts that have income above the statutory threshold amounts.

64. The answer is A. Lathan's partnership basis is increased to **$71,000** ($46,000 + $25,000 [25% × $100,000]). The partnership has four equal partners, so each would increase the basis of his partnership interest by his share of the debt (25% × $100,000).

65. The answer is C. Nicholas must report the $10,000 guaranteed payment as income. He is a 50% partner, so he must also report 50% of the partnership's income. The answer is calculated as follows: guaranteed payment ($10,000 + $21,000 [$42,000 × 50%]) = **$31,000**.

> **Note:** This question is somewhat tricky. Remember that the guaranteed payment has *already been deducted* in order to figure the partnership's ordinary income for the year. That is because the guaranteed payment is treated as an ordinary business deduction on Form 1065. For more information on the concept of guaranteed payments, see IRS publication 541, *Partnerships*.

66. The answer is D. Although personal exemptions are suspended for individuals until 2025, the personal exemptions available to trusts and estates are still allowed. Qualified Disability Trusts (QDTs) are unique. In 2021, a QDT is allowed an exemption of $4,300. This is the amount that individuals would have received as a personal exemption, had exemptions not been suspended by the TCJA. The exemption is allowed in full and is not subject to a phaseout. Qualified Disability Trusts are responsible for filing a yearly tax return, Form 1041.

67. The answer is C. A disregarded entity is a single-member limited liability company (SMLLC) that is disregarded for federal tax purposes. A domestic LLC with one member as an individual will be treated as a sole proprietorship, or "disregarded" as being separate from its owner for income tax purposes (but is still considered a separate entity for purposes of employment tax and certain excise taxes). An individual owner of a single-member LLC is subject to the tax on net earnings from self-employment in the same manner as a sole proprietorship. Furthermore, a domestic SMLLC with a sole corporate member will have its activities reported on the corporate member's own tax return.

68. The answer is A. Jonnie must report $10,000 of taxable partnership income in 2021, the year that the income was *earned*. After the distribution, his remaining partnership basis would be $500. Jonnie must report his share of partnership income in the year it is earned, regardless of the amounts actually distributed. The municipal bond interest is nontaxable interest, so it retains its character as nontaxable when it is distributed to Jonnie. However, the exempt income does increase Jonnie's basis in his partnership interest, so after the distribution he still has $500 in basis left. Since Jonnie had $10,000 of ordinary income from the partnership in 2021, he is required to report that amount in 2021, even if he did not receive it during the year. The answer is calculated as follows:

Jonnie's starting partnership basis	$0
Ordinary income	$10,000
Tax-exempt income	$1,500
Basis at the end of the year	**$11,500**
Cash distribution made in 2021	$11,000
Basis after cash distribution	**$500**

69. The answer is D. The answer is calculated as follows: **$24,960** ($24,000 + $960 sales tax). This is a barter transaction. Generally, the FMV of property exchanged for services is includable in income. The basis of property is usually its cost. However, if services are performed for a price **agreed on beforehand**, the price will be accepted as the FMV if there is no evidence to the contrary. Since Theodore charged $24,000 for his services and agreed to the transfer, $24,000 will be accepted as the FMV. The sales tax on a purchase is always added to the basis of an asset, capitalized, and depreciated. The basis of an asset also includes the following items:

- Freight in (shipping costs).
- Installation and testing.
- Excise taxes.
- Legal and accounting fees (when they must be capitalized).
- Real estate taxes (if assumed by the buyer for the seller).

70. The answer is D. Since the corporation is liquidating (essentially closing down its operations), the distribution is treated as a sale. Great Basin Corporation would recognize income of **$138,000** on the distribution ($200,000 FMW - $62,000 basis). A corporation recognizes gain or loss when it makes a *liquidating* distribution to its shareholders.

71. The answer is B. Because Trevor used the car 70% for business, he can deduct 70% of the auto expenses as a business expense. The answer is calculated as follows:

$$([\$235 + \$20 + \$25] = \$280) \times 70\% = \$196$$
$$\underline{(\$5,500 \times 70\%) = \$3,850}$$
Allowable expense: $4,046

72. The answer is C. A corporation whose S election is revoked or terminated must generally wait five years (60 months) before making an S election again. There are exceptions that allow for entities to elect S-status earlier than the mandatory five-year waiting period, but only with IRS consent.

73. The answer is B. Kistar Corporation may claim a **$6,500** dividends-received deduction ($10,000 x 65%). The DRD is calculated like this:

Percentage of Ownership in Distributing Corporation	Dividends Received Deduction %
Less than 20%	50%
At least 20%, but less than 80%	65%
80% or more	100%

This deduction applies to dividends from corporations that have at least 20% of their stock owned by the recipient corporation. Only C Corporations may claim the dividends-received deduction.

74. The answer is D. Fees that have been paid to attorneys for work on behalf of the estate (or amounts that can reasonably be expected to be paid) may be claimed as a deduction against the value of the estate on Form 706. Answer "C" is incorrect, because federal estate taxes are never deductible on the estate tax return. Answer "A" is incorrect, because the deduction for property taxes is limited to the taxes accrued before the date of the decedent's death (not after). Answer "B" is incorrect, because daycare expenses incurred after Connor's death would not be deductible as expenses of the estate. The following deductions are allowable from the gross estate:

- Marital Deduction: All the property that passes to a surviving spouse (who is a U.S. citizen) is eligible for the marital deduction.
- Charitable Deduction: If the decedent leaves property to a qualifying charity, it is deductible from the gross estate.
- Unpaid mortgages and outstanding debts.
- Administration fees and legal expenses of the estate.
- Losses during estate administration.
- Funeral expenses of the deceased.

75. The answer is A. A trademark is not eligible for Section 179, because it is classified under IRC Section 197 as an "intangible asset." A business must amortize the cost of "Section 197 intangibles" over 15 years. The following assets are Section 197 intangibles and must be amortized over 15 years (180 months):

- Goodwill, going concern value, and any workforce in place.
- Business books and records, operating systems, or any other information base, including lists or other information concerning current or prospective customers.
- A patent, copyright, formula, process, design, or similar item.
- A customer-based or supplier-based intangible.
- A license, permit, or other right granted by the government (such as a liquor license).
- A covenant not to compete entered into in connection with the acquisition of a trade or business.
- Any franchise, trademark, or trade name.
- A contract for the use of, or a term interest in, any item in this list.

Answer "B" is incorrect, because business vehicles can qualify for Section 179. Answer "C" and "D" are incorrect, because the Section 179 deduction is allowable on new and used equipment, as well as off-the-shelf software.

76. The answer is D. Easton Auto Parts' final return is due by November 15, 2021. It will cover the short period from January 1, 2021, through July 12, 2021. November 15 is the fifteenth day of the *fourth* month following the close of the corporation's tax year, which was a short year because the corporation dissolved (stopped doing business).

77. The answer is A. In this case, Gabe is considered to constructively own 100% of the partnership, because the rules for constructive ownership consider the ownership of his family members, which only includes children, brothers, sisters, spouses, ancestors, and *lineal* descendants (like a grandson or granddaughter). This rule does not apply to cousins or step-siblings (or any other step-relationships, like a step-father or step-mother; they are not considered "related parties" for the purposes of this rule). Therefore, his ownership is calculated as follows:

Gabe	20%
Gabe's son	20%
Gabe's brother	60%
Gabe's "Constructive Ownership"	**100%**

78. The answer is A. Brett must report a capital gain of $6,000 on his tax return ($30,000 - $24,000 = $6,000). A shareholder's stock basis cannot go below zero. Therefore, if a nondividend distribution is made *in excess* of stock basis, the distribution is taxed as a capital gain on the shareholder's return.

79. The answer is C. A SIMPLE 401(k) plan may offer participant loans (although the employer is not required to do so).[13] Loans are not permitted from IRAs or from IRA-based plans such as SEPs, traditional IRAs and SIMPLE IRA plans. Borrowing money from an IRA is considered a "prohibited transaction." If the owner of an IRA "borrows" from an IRA, the IRA is no longer an IRA, and the value of the entire IRA is included in the owner's income.

80. The answer is D. For the sale of livestock due to weather-related conditions in an area eligible for federal disaster assistance, the replacement period ends *four years* after the close of the first tax year in which the taxpayer realizes any part of his gain from the sale or exchange of livestock. So, Tripp would have **four years** to purchase "replacement livestock" and not recognize a taxable gain from the insurance reimbursement. Generally speaking, a "disaster loss" is a loss that occurred in a federally declared disaster area because of a federally declared disaster. Although a disaster loss is a *type* of casualty loss, special rules apply that provide more favorable tax treatment for disaster losses.

81. The answer is D. Sunway Engineering, LLP must include the fair market value of the items it received in exchange for services. This is considered "bartering income," and it is treated the same as if the partnership had received cash. Therefore, the answer is $8,000 machinery + $3,000 design services = **$11,000**.

---

[13] A qualified plan may, but is not required to, provide for participant loans. If a plan provides for loans, the plan may limit the amount that can be taken as a loan. Loans are only possible from qualified plans that satisfy the requirements of 401(a), from annuity plans such as 403(a) or 403(b), and from governmental plans. For more information, see official IRS guidance here: https://www.irs.gov/retirement-plans/retirement-plans-faqs-regarding-loans

82. The answer is A. Schein Accountancy, LLP will not owe income tax, because it is a pass-through entity. A partnership does not pay income tax. However, a partnership can still be liable for other taxes, such as employment taxes (FUTA, Social Security, Medicare taxes) and excise taxes.

83. The answer is D. Health insurance premiums for a self-employed taxpayer are not deductible on Schedule C. Self-employed taxpayers may potentially deduct up to 100% of their medical insurance premiums, but only as an adjustment to income on Schedule 1 of Form 1040. This deduction is also limited by self-employment and taxable income. So, for example, if the business has an overall loss for the year, the health insurance premiums would not be deductible.

84. The answer is B. An exchange of an undeveloped lot for a factory building would be a qualifying exchange. The other answers are all prohibited under the section 1031 rules.[14] Answer "C" is incorrect, because the exchange of a personal home for business property is not a valid exchange. In order for a like-kind exchange to be valid, both properties must be used in a business or held for investment. Most real property is qualifying property, *unless* it is personal-use. For example, real property that is improved may be exchanged for vacant land. Answer "A" is incorrect because real estate within the United States cannot be exchanged for foreign real estate outside the United States. Answer "D" is incorrect because only real property qualifies for like-kind exchange treatment, so cryptocurrency would not qualify. A taxpayer reports a section 1031 exchange on Form 8824, *Like-Kind Exchanges.*

85. The answer is C. The TCJA eliminated business deductions for the cost of providing qualified employee transportation fringe benefits, such as: transit passes, qualified parking, light-rail passes, etc., *unless* the expenses are necessary for an employee's safety. Transportation benefits are still non-taxable to the employee, but the business can no longer deduct them, unless the amount is included in the employee's W-2 income as wages. This is true even if the business has an accountable plan.

86. The answer is A. Culver Packard Inc. must recognize a taxable gain of **$60,000**. This transaction is treated as a **sale**. It is as if Culver Packard Inc. sold the building for $250,000 and used the profits from the sale to pay the debt. Culver Packard Inc. must realize a taxable gain as if the property had been sold at its fair market value and the proceeds from the sale were used to pay off the creditor.

87. The answer is D. If a business activity reports a net profit at least *three out of the last five* years, including the current year, the IRS presumes that the activity is engaged in for profit, rather than a hobby. This rule changes to two out of the last seven years for equine-related activities; for example, racing, breeding, and training horses.

88. The answer is B. Assessments for local improvements are items that tend to increase the value of property, such as streets and sidewalks, and are added to the basis of a taxpayer's property. These items cannot be deducted as taxes or as an expense. However, a business can deduct assessments for local benefits if they are for maintenance and repairs. A business may also deduct any interest charges that are related to the improvements.

---

14 The Tax Cuts and Jobs Act modified the law for Section 1031 exchanges. The nonrecognition of gain or loss in like-kind exchanges of property used in a trade or business or for investment is limited to real property only (real estate). However, real property inside the U.S. cannot be exchanged for real property outside the U.S.

89. The answer is D. The entire meal amount is a qualified business expense. In 2021, business meals provided by a restaurant are 100% deductible. Sadie can deduct the full amount of travel expense (the taxi cab fare). Therefore, the deductible expense is calculated as follows: $250 + $10 = **$260.**

90. The answer is C. The normal due date for Form 1041 is the fifteenth day of the fourth month following the end of the entity's tax year (unless it falls on a weekend or holiday). For the 2021 tax year, the due date is April 18, 2022 (the same as individual returns). An extension of five-and-a-half months can be requested if Form 7004 is filed. The tax year of an estate may be either a calendar or a fiscal year, subject to the election made at the time the first return is filed. An election will also be made on the first return as to method (cash, accrual, or other) to report an estate's ongoing taxable income. Form 1041 must be filed for any domestic estate that has gross income for the tax year of $600 or more, or a beneficiary who is a nonresident alien (with any amount of income).

> **Note:** April 18, 2022 is the deadline for 2021 returns, due to the Emancipation Day holiday in Washington DC.

91. The answer is D. Keller must file Form 8300, *Report of Cash Payments Over $10,000 Received in a Trade or Business.* When a business receives a cash payment of more than $10,000 from one transaction or from two or more related transactions, the business must file Form 8300. The requirement also applies to certain monetary instruments, such as traveler's checks, bank drafts, cashier's checks, and money orders. The form requires the name, address, and Social Security number of the buyer. The reporting requirement is designed to combat money laundering. This provision does not apply to personal checks or bank wire transfers.

> **Note:** The filing requirements for Form 8300 do *not* apply to personal transactions, only business-related transactions.

92. The answer is D. Corporate dividends and distributions to shareholders will decrease E&P. The amount of a C corporation's earnings and profits determines the tax treatment of corporate distributions to shareholders. The starting point for determining corporate E&P is the corporation's taxable income. The following transactions *increase* the amount of E&P:

- Long-term contracts reported on the completed contract method.
- Intangible drilling costs deducted currently.
- Mine exploration and development costs deducted currently.
- Dividends-received deduction.

The following transactions *reduce* the amount of E&P:

- Corporate federal income taxes.
- Life insurance policy premiums on a corporate officer.
- Excess charitable contributions (over the 10% allowable limit).
- Expenses relating to tax-exempt income.
- Excess of capital losses over capital gains.
- Corporate dividends and other distributions to shareholders.

93. The answer is B. Fruitman Cannery, Inc. can take a deduction for the interest paid on the loan. However, the sales tax is not currently deductible. It must be added to the cost of the depreciable asset and depreciated over its useful life. If the business otherwise qualifies, Fruitman Cannery may be able to take section 179 or bonus depreciation on the purchase.

94. The answer is B. Because the cash received does not exceed the basis of her partnership interest, Deborah does not recognize any gain on the distribution. Any gain on the land will be recognized when she later sells or disposes of it. The distributions decrease the adjusted basis of her partnership interest to **$57,000** ($165,000 - [$80,000 cash + $28,000 machinery (the partnership's adjusted basis in the property)]).

95. The answer is D. The amount of current earnings and profits that is allocated to Kayla is $32,000 ($64,000 earnings × 50% stock ownership). Kayla must report dividend income of **$32,000.** The remaining amount of the distribution ($40,000 - $32,000 = $8,000) is treated as a return of capital and reduces Kayla's stock basis to **$42,000** ($50,000 - $8,000). Corporate distributions are treated as dividends to the extent of the shareholder's share of corporate earnings and profits.

96. The answer is B. Melanie drives a total of 33 miles each workday, but only **18 miles** are deductible as a business expense. It is 10 miles from her home to the first office and 5 miles from the last office back home. These first 15 miles are commuting miles and, therefore, not deductible. It is 13 miles from the first office to the second office and 5 miles from the second office to the third office (see diagram below). [This question is based on an example in the IRS official VITA training guide.]

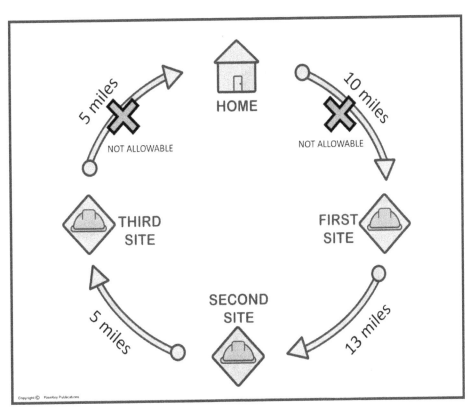

63

97. The answer is C. Cascade Partnership is required to use April 30 as its tax year-end. A partnership generally must conform its tax year to its partners' tax years. If one (or any partners that have the same tax year) own a majority interest (an interest in partnership profits and capital of more than 50%), the partnership must use the tax year of those partners. In this case, since Daisy Corporation and Maxim Corporation share the same tax year and their combined partnership interest exceeds 50%, Cascade Partnership is required to use April 30 as its tax year-end.

98. The answer is D. A "controlled group" is a group of corporations that are related through common ownership, typically as either parent-subsidiary or brother-sister corporations. A parent-subsidiary controlled group involves a parent corporation that owns at least 80% of the voting power of at least one other corporation (with possible additional corporations that are at least 80% owned by either the common parent or one of the subsidiary entities). A brother-sister controlled group involves situations in which five or fewer individuals, estates, or trusts own 80% or more of the combined voting power for multiple corporations, and have identical common ownership within the individual corporations of at least 50%. Members of controlled groups are subject to rules regarding related party transactions that may require deferral of recognition for losses or expenses incurred by one party.

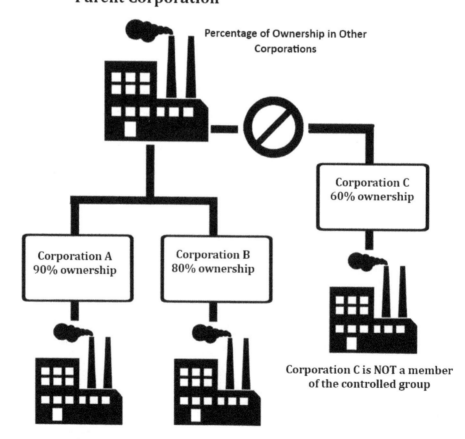

Example of a Parent-Subsidiary Controlled Group

Parent Corporation

99. The answer is A. Pioneer's cost of goods sold is calculated as follows:

Beginning inventory balance		$1,200,000
Manufacturing costs		
	Raw materials purchases	5,400,000
	Freight-in charges	175,000
	Manufacturing wages and benefits	4,025,000
	Other direct manufacturing costs	875,000
	Minus the ending inventory balance	(1,575,000)
COGS		**$10,100,000**

The other costs outlined in the question are not used in the manufacturing process, and therefore are not included in the calculation of cost of goods sold.

100. The answer is D. Most employers pay both Federal unemployment taxes (FUTA) as well as state unemployment taxes. The FUTA tax rate is 6.0%. The tax applies to the first $7,000 a business pays to each employee as wages during the year. The $7,000 is often referred to as the "FUTA wage base." Only the employer pays FUTA tax, it is never imposed on the employee.

#2 Sample Exam: Businesses

(Please test yourself first; then check the correct answers at the end of this exam.)

1. Teddy is a popular comedian who files on Schedule C. He has three employees: a full-time secretary and two part-time assistants who manage his website and club bookings. During the tax year, Teddy has the following meal and entertainment expenses related to his business:

Expense	Cost
Tickets to a golfing tournament with a club owner	$240
Business meals at restaurants	152
Snacks and beverages for the employee break room	260
Office party for Teddy's employees and their families	552

Based on the information above, what is the dollar amount of Teddy's deductible expense on his Schedule C?

A. $379
B. $482
C. $758
D. $834

2. Phillip is a real estate professional who owns and manages several rental properties. During the tax year, Phillip exchanges a residential rental property with an adjusted basis of $50,000 and a fair market value of $205,000 for an undeveloped parcel of farmland with a fair market value of $399,000. The farmland is worth more than the rental property, so to complete the transaction, Phillip pays additional cash of $194,000 for the farmland. The transaction qualifies for section 1031 exchange treatment. Once the exchange is completed, what is Phillip's basis in the farmland?

A. $50,000
B. $230,000
C. $244,000
D. $399,000

3. Benicio is a full-time life insurance sales agent. His employer issues him a Form W-2, but Benicio reports his income on Schedule C. For federal tax purposes, Benicio is considered what type of worker?

A. An independent contractor.
B. A contract employee.
C. A statutory nonemployee.
D. A statutory employee.

4. Which of the following businesses, if operated as a sole proprietorship, would be classified as a "Specified Service Trade or Business" for the purposes of determining eligibility for the section 199A tax deduction for Qualified Business Income?

A. Accounting Firm.
B. Engineering Firm.
C. Farming business.
D. Licensed realtor.

5. The cash method of accounting can be used by all of the following entities except:

A. An S corporation that produces inventory, with $5,000,000 of annual gross receipts.
B. A tax shelter with $100,000 of annual gross receipts.
C. A family farming corporation with $20 million of annual gross receipts.
D. A partnership with a corporate partner with $24 million in average annual gross receipts for the three previous years.

6. Dewey is a self-employed dog groomer. Which of the following expenses would *not* be deductible on his Schedule C?

A. Mileage expenses.
B. Interest paid on business loans.
C. Expenses for a home office.
D. HSA contributions.

7. What is an advantage of an S corporation over a general partnership?

A. More flexibility.
B. Liability protection.
C. Pass-through entity.
D. No entity-level income tax.

8. Lorex Chemicals, Inc. is a C corporation. The company purchased an office building for $940,000 several years ago. Lorex Chemicals made substantial improvements to the building at a cost of $40,000 and deducted depreciation of $48,000 over the years. In 2021, Lorex Chemicals sold the building for $2,000,000 cash and also received equipment from the buyer with a fair market value of $400,000. The buyer paid Lorex Chemicals' outstanding real estate taxes of $6,000 and assumed an existing mortgage of $340,000 on the building. Lorex Chemicals immediately invested the proceeds in another building. What is Lorex Chemicals' taxable gain on the sale, if any?

A. $0
B. $1,718,000
C. $1,814,000
D. $1,820,000

9. Willard is the single owner of an LLC that provides party planning services. Absent any elections, how will Willard's LLC be treated for federal tax purposes?

A. Partnership.
B. C corporation.
C. S corporation.
D. Disregarded entity.

10. Which of the following is NOT an acceptable inventory method?

A. Specific Identification.
B. Cost-Price.
C. Last-In, First Out (LIFO).
D. First-In, First-Out (FIFO).

11. Which of the following entities is *prohibited* from being classified as a partnership for tax purposes?

A. A tax-exempt organization.
B. A small law firm with two individual owners.
C. An LLC with three members, one of whom is an estate.
D. A business venture with spousal co-owners.

12. For Federal Insurance Contributions Act (FICA tax) purposes, all of the following types of income are taxed as wages *except*:

A. A signing bonus upon hire for a new job.
B. Vacation pay due to employer separation.
C. Severance pay due to workforce reduction.
D. Reimbursements under an employer accountable plan.

13. According to the IRS, in order to be deductible, a business expense must be *both*:

A. "Ordinary" and "necessary".
B. "Usual" and "customary".
C. "Beneficial" and "customary".
D. "Substantiated" and "necessary".

14. When does a corporation formally adopt its tax year?

A. On the date that the business is formally incorporated.
B. Within 2½ months of its incorporation.
C. When it files its first income tax return.
D. By the end of the first month following the date of incorporation.

15. Jane Johnson died two years ago. Jane was a well-known author, and her books continue to generate revenue after her death. Her estate is currently going through its period of administration. In 2021, the Estate of Jane Johnson realized $30,000 of business income from the sale of Jane's books. The estate has two beneficiaries, Jane's sons, Bradley and Nestor. The executor of the estate is Jane's trusted attorney. The executor distributed $10,000 of the business income to Nestor, and $20,000 to Jane's other son, Bradley, based on their relative share of the estate as heirs. The allowable depreciation on the estate's business property is $3,000 in 2021. Ignoring any other deductions or items of income, how should the depreciation be allocated to the beneficiaries?

A. Nestor can take a depreciation deduction of $1,000; Bradley can take a deduction of $2,000.
B. The depreciation must be divided equally between the beneficiaries. Nestor can take a depreciation deduction of $1,500, and Bradley can take a deduction of $1,500.
C. Neither beneficiary can take a deduction for depreciation, but the estate can take a depreciation deduction on Form 1041.
D. Neither the estate or the beneficiaries can take a depreciation deduction until all the assets of the estate are distributed.

16. Worldwide Trucking, Inc. is a transportation business that pays fuel excise taxes. How should these taxes be treated for IRS purposes?

A. Excise taxes are not a deductible business expense.
B. Excise taxes may be currently deductible or subject to capitalization.
C. Excise taxes must be capitalized.
D. Excise taxes may be deductible to corporations, but not to individual taxpayers.

17. MedChem Pharmaceuticals, Inc. has twenty-five employees. During the year, MedChem Pharmaceuticals pays its full-time secretary, Michelle, various fringe benefits. Which of the following fringe benefits would *not* be reported on Michelle's Form W-2?

A. A retroactive wage increase.
B. Payment for sick leave.
C. Mileage reimbursements made under an accountable plan.
D. The portion of group-term life insurance that exceeds the cost of $50,000 of coverage.

18. Bobby and Sienna are married. Both are self-employed and run their own businesses. Each is enrolled in a self-only HDHP (high deductible health plan). Can Bobby and Sienna set up a joint HSA, even though they have separate businesses?

A. They can set up a joint HSA, but only if they file jointly.
B. They can set up a joint HSA, whether they file jointly or separately.
C. They can set up a joint HSA if they designate the HSA as a "family plan."
D. They cannot set up a joint HSA.

19. All of the following items would be included in the gross receipts of a business for a tax year *except*:

A. Sales made but income not collected during the tax year for a business using an accrual accounting method.
B. Sales taxes collected by a business using the cash accounting method in a state where sales tax is imposed on the buyer, and the seller is collecting the sales tax as an agent of the state.
C. The fair market value of property the business received in exchange for a good or service bartered.
D. Lease bonus and lease cancellation payments received from a lessee renting personal property or real estate.

20. Which of the following entities may be subject to the *unrelated business income tax* (UBIT)?

A. A qualified disability trust.
B. A bankruptcy estate.
C. A C corporation.
D. A tax-exempt organization.

21. What is the federal income tax rate for a C corporation?

A. 10%
B. 21%
C. 35%
D. 37%

22. Which of the following would NOT be classified as a partnership distribution?

A. A year-end bonus paid to an employee of the partnership.
B. A withdrawal by a partner in anticipation of the current year's earnings.
C. A complete or partial liquidation of a partner's interest.
D. A distribution to all partners in a complete liquidation of the partnership.

23. Sophia and Logan formed the Econix Corporation in 2021. As part of the capitalization of the newly-formed corporation, Sophia contributed $500,000 of cash, and Logan contributed land and a building with a fair market value of $700,000 and an adjusted basis of $450,000. Logan received $200,000 of cash from the corporation when the land and building were contributed. Sophia and Logan each receive 50% of the corporate stock after these contributions. What is the tax basis of the land and building to Econix Corporation?

A. $250,000
B. $500,000
C. $650,000
D. $700,000

24. Carey is a self-employed soybean farmer whose crops were wiped out by a flood. He receives $115,000 of crop insurance payments in 2021 due to the disaster. He reports his income and loss on Schedule F. What method of accounting must he use in order to postpone recognizing the gain in 2021?

A. Accrual method.
B. Crop method.
C. Hybrid method.
D. Cash method.

25. Karen is a licensed chiropractor. She forms an LLC during the year and elects to have the LLC taxed as an S corporation. What is the correct procedure for making this election?

A. The LLC must file Form 8832.
B. The LLC must file Form 2553.
C. The LLC must file both Form 8832 and Form 1120S.
D. The LLC must file Form 1120S and elect S corporation status with its first tax return.

26. Boggle Corporation trades an office complex with an adjusted basis of $300,000 and a fair market value of $680,000 for a factory building in a qualified section 1031 exchange. The original cost of the office complex was $500,000, and it had $200,000 of accumulated depreciation. Boggle Co. also paid $80,000 of additional cash (boot) to obtain the new property. The factory building has a fair market value of $750,000 at the time of the exchange. What is Boggle Corporation's adjusted basis in the factory building *after* the 1031 exchange?

A. $240,000
B. $380,000
C. $670,000
D. $760,000

27. Travis is a self-employed farmer who files a Schedule F. On February 1, 2021, a vandal destroyed a large tractor on Travis' farm with a pipe bomb. The tractor could not be repaired and was considered a total loss. After a period of negotiations, Travis' insurance company compensated him for the full amount of the loss. He received the insurance check on November 2, 2021. The tractor's adjusted basis is zero. How long does Travis have to purchase a replacement tractor under the rules for involuntary conversions to defer any potential gain?

A. February 1, 2024.
B. November 2, 2023.
C. December 31, 2022.
D. December 31, 2023.

28. A C corporation that does not file its tax return by the due date may be penalized 5% of the unpaid tax for each month or part of a month the return is late, up to a maximum _____ of the unpaid tax.

A. 25%
B. 50%
C. 75%
D. 100%

29. Which of the following taxpayers is generally considered self-employed?

A. A statutory employee.
B. An executor of an estate who is also a family member of the deceased.
C. A sole shareholder of an S corporation.
D. A general partner in a partnership.

30. Sutton is a self-employed architect. In 2021, he had gross receipts of $100,053 for his business. He incurred supply expenses of $17,750 and $400 in business meals at restaurants. Sutton also entertained a wealthy client at a baseball game. The cost was $350 for two tickets. His written mileage log shows he drove 2,600 business miles. He uses the standard mileage rate to determine his driving expenses. How much can he deduct for his total business expenses on Schedule C?

A. $17,750
B. $19,445
C. $19,606
D. $20,950

31. In determining whether a worker is an employee or an independent contractor, the IRS will evaluate the following factors:

A. Behavioral control.
B. Financial control.
C. Type of relationship.
D. All of the above.

32. Donna transfers a parcel of land worth $145,000 with an adjusted basis of $100,000 and renders web design services valued at $15,000 to Hubbel Group, Inc. in exchange for stock valued at $160,000. Right after the transfer, Donna owns 90% of the outstanding stock in Hubbel Group Inc. What is the taxable effect of this transaction on Donna?

A. Donna recognizes $15,000 of ordinary income.
B. Donna does not recognize gain or loss.
C. Donna recognizes $30,000 of ordinary income.
D. Donna recognizes $15,000 of ordinary income and $15,000 of capital gain income.

33. Chateau Winery, Inc. is a cash basis C corporation. The business made regular estimated payments throughout the year based on its current-year tax liability. On October 16, 2021, the company suffers a financial loss when a bad storm destroys one of its vineyards. After this event, Chateau Winery expects to have a loss for the year, and it could really use the overpaid taxes in December to defray disaster recovery costs. How can the corporation obtain a quick refund of its overpaid estimated taxes?

A. The business must file its corporate return (Form 1120) to receive a refund.
B. The business can file Form 4466, to obtain an overpayment of its estimated tax.
C. The business can contact EFTPS and request a refund of its estimated tax.
D. The business can contact the Taxpayer Advocate Service.

34. Pauly sells weight-loss supplements. He reports his income and loss on Schedule C. During the current year, Pauly took $425 worth of supplements out of his inventory for his own personal use. What is the proper tax treatment of this action?

A. He must reduce the amount of his total inventory purchases by $425.
B. As a bodybuilder, he deducts the cost of the supplements as a medical expense.
C. He must increase the cost of his inventory by the value of the personal use items.
D. He can deduct the cost of the supplements as an advertising expense.

35. Which of the following businesses would NOT be potentially subject to the Uniform Capitalization Rules, regardless of the business' gross receipts?

A. A business that produces inventory for sale to customers.
B. A realty business that acquires land for resale.
C. Creative expenses incurred by a self-employed writer.
D. A farming business that raises beef cattle for resale.

36. The annual reporting period for a business' income tax return is called a _____.

A. Reporting year.
B. Accounting year.
C. Fiscal year.
D. Tax year.

37. Gentlemanly Menswear, Inc. is a clothing manufacturer that sells designer men's suits. Which of the following is not a cost that goes into figuring the company's cost of goods sold?

A. The cost of producing men's suits.
B. Storage costs for completed suits that have not been shipped yet.
C. Factory overhead.
D. Product advertising.

38. Danika is a licensed real estate agent who works for a single realty firm. Payments for her services are directly related to her real estate sales. She has a written contract that specifies she will not be treated as an employee for federal tax purposes. What is Danika's worker classification?

A. An independent shareholder.
B. A statutory employee.
C. A statutory non-employee.
D. A common law employee.

39. If a business accumulates $100,000 or more in payroll taxes during a deposit period, when is it required to deposit the tax?

A. By the next business day.
B. Monthly.
C. Weekly.
D. Quarterly.

40. In which of the following scenarios is a business required to obtain prior IRS approval?

A. An existing business wishes to change from the cash method to the accrual method.
B. Correcting a math error or an error in figuring tax liability.
C. Changing the accounting method when the change is required by tax law.
D. Changing a business' legal name.

41. Windsor Windows, Inc. is a calendar-year C corporation that sells window coverings and draperies. Windsor has a net short-term capital gain of $3,000 and a net long-term capital loss of $11,000. What is the proper treatment of these transactions?

A. The short-term gain offsets some of the long-term loss, leaving a net capital loss of $8,000. The loss can be claimed against ordinary income.
B. The short-term gain offsets some of the long-term loss, leaving a net capital loss of $8,000. The corporation treats this $8,000 as a short-term loss when carried back or forward.
C. Windsor has a net long-term capital loss of $11,000. Any gains would be ordinary income.
D. Windsor has a net short-term capital gain of $3,000. The losses are not deductible by the corporation, but they can be passed through to the shareholders.

42. Which of the following will disqualify a corporation from electing S corporation status?

A. Issuance of voting and non-voting stock.
B. Having 101 unrelated shareholders.
C. The stock is issued to an Electing Small Business Trust (ESBT).
D. A shareholder dies, and the stock passes to a domestic estate.

43. Suzanne is a partner in two different construction businesses. She is a 70% owner in the Concrete Partnership and a 51% owner in the Wolker Partnership. During the tax year, the Concrete Partnership sold a cement mixer to the Wolker Partnership for $60,000. At the time of the sale, the cement mixer had an adjusted basis of $95,000 to the Concrete Partnership and a fair market value of $110,000. What is the amount of loss that the Concrete Partnership can recognize on this sale?

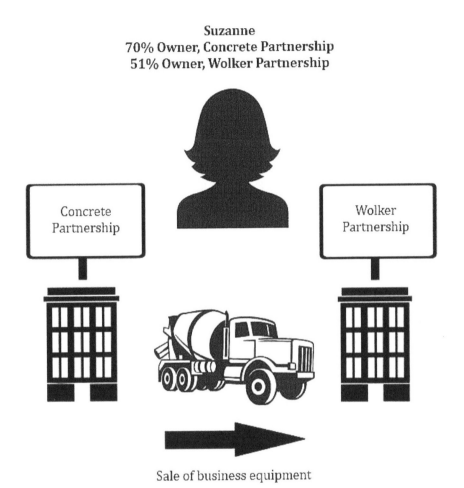

Sale of business equipment

A. $0
B. $15,000
C. $35,000
D. $50,000

44. Which of the following business types generally does not have to use a "required" tax year?

A. Partnership.
B. S corporation.
C. Sole proprietorship.
D. C corporation.

45. Which of the following assets would *not* be classified as a section 197 asset?

A. Goodwill.
B. Partnership interest.
C. Franchise rights.
D. Workforce in place.

46. How many years should an employer keep employment tax records, such as copies of Forms W-2?

A. One year.
B. Three years.
C. Four years.
D. Ten years.

47. Sachs Group, Inc. is a publicly-traded corporation with audited financial statements. The company has a formal accounting procedure in place to expense the cost of tangible property. Under the *de minimis expense safe harbor* of the final tangible property regulations, Sachs Group Inc. can choose to deduct items that cost up to _____ per invoice or item.

A. $200
B. $500
C. $2,500
D. $5,000

48. An S corporation stockholder's basis is generally *increased* by which of the following?

A. Taxable income.
B. Nontaxable discharge of indebtedness.
C. Separately stated loss items.
D. Distributions.

49. The Paskins Partnership has four equal partners, each owning a 25% stake in the partnership. The Paskins Partnership would like to **elect-out** of the centralized partnership audit regime (CPAR) on its 2021 tax return. Which of the following partners would disqualify the Paskins Partnership from making this election?

A. Jeffrey, an individual taxpayer who holds his partnership interest directly.
B. The Estate of Melvin Jones, the estate of a deceased partner.
C. Tamara, who owns her partnership interest through a grantor trust.
D. Brandywine Corporation, an S corporation.

50. The computation of recapture amounts is not necessary when the business use percentage of section 179 or listed property exceeds what threshold?

A. 10%
B. 25%
C. 45%
D. 50%

51. McCarthy Accountancy, Inc. reimburses one of its auditors for meals using the federal *per diem* rate while the employee is away from home on an auditing assignment. How should McCarthy Accountancy treat this cost on its business return?

A. The business may deduct 0% of the per diem amounts on its tax return.
B. The business may deduct 50% of the per diem amounts on its tax return.
C. The business may deduct 80% of the per diem amounts on its tax return.
D. The business may deduct 100% of the per diem amounts on its tax return.

52. An exempt organization may qualify under section 501(c)(3) if it is organized exclusively for which of the following purposes?

A. Charitable purposes.
B. Economic interests.
C. Political action committee.
D. Homeowners' association.

53. Generally, a "fiscal year" is 12 consecutive months ending on the last day of any month except _____.

A. January
B. March
C. April
D. December

54. Bargain Retail Corp. employs 40 full-time sales employees. They also have 20 part-time employees working an average of 20 hours per week. How many full-time *equivalent* employees does Bargain Retail Corp have for ACA purposes, and is the company considered an "Applicable Large Employer" (ALE) for tax purposes?

A. Bargain Retail has only 40 full-time employees; it is NOT an Applicable Large Employer.
B. Bargain Retail has 45 full-time equivalent employees; it is NOT an Applicable Large Employer.
C. Bargain Retail has 50 full-time equivalent employees; it is considered an Applicable Large Employer.
D. Bargain Retail has 60 full-time equivalent employees; it is considered an Applicable Large Employer.

55. If a C corporation makes a below-market rate loan to one of its shareholders, the corporation generally is deemed to make a payment to the shareholder. How is this "deemed payment" treated for federal tax purposes if the shareholder is not an employee?

A. As a gift.
B. As a dividend.
C. As interest.
D. As wages.

56. All of the following are true regarding Income in Respect of a Decedent (IRD) *except*:

A. IRD is income the decedent would have received had death not occurred.
B. The character of IRD remains the same as it would have been to the decedent.
C. If an individual receives IRD and includes it on their return, they are not allowed to claim a deduction for the estate tax paid on that income if Form 706 was filed.
D. IRD must be included as income on *either* (1) the decedent's estate return, if the estate receives it, or (2) any person to whom the estate properly distributes the right to receive it.

57. Hillenbrand Foods, Inc. is an accrual-basis, calendar-year C corporation. For tax year 2021, Hillenbrand Foods has taxable income of $105,000 *before* considering charitable contributions. On December 15, 2021, the board of directors authorizes a $30,000 charitable contribution to a qualified 501(c)(3) charity. What is the *last day* that Hillenbrand Foods can make this charitable contribution and still take the expense on its 2021 tax return, and what is the amount of their allowable charitable deduction on Form 1120?

Last Date for Contribution	Allowable Deduction
A. December 31, 2021	$30,000
B. October 17, 2022	$26,250
C. March 15, 2022	$10,500
D. April 18, 2022	$26,250

58. Christopher is a full-time life insurance salesman. He is classified as a statutory employee and receives $90,000 in wages during 2021. He has no other income for the year. Does Christopher qualify for the QBI deduction?

A. No, he does not qualify because wages do not qualify as QBI.
B. Yes, Christopher qualifies for the QBI deduction, because he is a statutory employee.
C. Christopher may qualify for the QBI deduction only if he sets up an LLC for his insurance activities.
D. There is not enough information to answer.

59. Jeffrey is a sole proprietor who owns a small timber farm. He reports his income and loss on Schedule F. He does not have any employees. Which of the following expenses would be allowed on Schedule F as a business expense?

A. Premiums paid for medical insurance.
B. Self-employment tax deduction.
C. Depreciation expense.
D. Health savings account deduction.

60. Edmund used his car only for personal purposes during the first six months of the year and incurred 3,400 miles on the car. For the last six months of the year, he drove the car a total of 18,000 miles. Of those miles, 16,000 were driven providing transportation through a popular ride-sharing service. He also incurred an additional $256 in parking fees and tolls during that time. He received a Form 1099-K showing the income he earned from the ride-sharing business and he will file a Schedule C. He plans to take the standard mileage rate. What is his allowable deduction for mileage in 2021?

A. $7,200
B. $8,960
C. $9,216
D. $10,606

61. Calvin is a licensed barber and owns the most popular barbershop in town. Calvin gives the following gifts to his best clients during the year:

- $50 box of cigars to client #1.
- $45 bottle of fine brandy to client #2.
- $30 silk tie to client #3.

He spent an additional $65 on packaging and shipping the gifts. What amount can Calvin deduct for his business-related gifts?

A. $125
B. $140
C. $153
D. $190

62. What is the deadline to file Form 5500, *Annual Return/Report of Employee Benefit Plan?*

A. The fifteenth day of the fourth month after the end of the plan year.
B. The fifteenth day of the fifth month after the end of the plan year.
C. The fifteenth day of the seventh month after the end of the plan year.
D. The last day of the seventh month after the end of the plan year.

63. James works as a self-employed carpenter. He has a truck that he uses exclusively for work. In order to deduct his business miles, what type of recordkeeping is required?

A. If the truck is 100% business use, then no recordkeeping is required.
B. He must keep a basic calendar of his driving locations.
C. He must keep written notes describing the business location.
D. He must keep a detailed mileage log for all business trips.

64. Through a medical practice broker, Kaplan Podiatry, Inc. purchased Coastal Podiatry. The goodwill and "going concern value" associated with the business purchase totaled $179,000. Over what number of years must the goodwill and "going concern value" be amortized by Kaplan Podiatry, Inc.?

A. 5 years.
B. 10 years.
C. 15 years.
D. 20 years.

65. Port Express, Inc. is an accrual-basis C Corporation. The company discovers an error in the useful life of a depreciable asset, a water vessel used as a ferry. The ferry should have been depreciated over ten years rather than seven years. The ferry was placed in service over five years ago. The ferry originally cost $124,000 and depreciation deductions currently total $63,000. What is the proper treatment of this error?

A. Port Express must amend all its prior returns to correct this depreciation error.
B. Port Express should file Form 3115 and claim the section 481(a) adjustment to correct the error.
C. Port Express does not have to get IRS consent to correct the depreciation error.
D. Port Express must recognize additional gain when the property is sold.

66. A C corporation can deduct all the following taxes as a business expense except:

A. State corporate franchise taxes.
B. Federal income taxes.
C. State income taxes.
D. Local income taxes.

67. Businesses must make sure that workers are properly classified. Businesses use several factors to determine how to classify their workers. Which of the following would *not* be a factor when determining whether a worker is an employee or an independent contractor?

A. Behavioral control
B. Financial control
C. The worker's age
D. Relationship of the Parties

68. Bonnie owns a hostel that she rents out to travelers. She had the following asset purchases in 2021. Ignoring any income limitations, what amount can Bonnie deduct under section 179?

- New HVAC system: $4,500.
- Beds and other furniture: $12,000.
- Appliances: $3,250.

A. $0
B. $4,500
C. $15,250
D. $19,750

69. Josephine is a self-employed consultant. During the tax year, Josephine drives a total of 18,000 miles. Of those miles, 8,000 were for her consulting business, 1,000 were personal miles, and 9,000 were miles that she incurred while volunteering for a qualified charity. She also incurred $250 worth of parking fees and tolls while meeting with her business clients in another city. What is her allowable deduction for transportation expenses on her Schedule C?

A. $4,280
B. $4,730
C. $5,100
D. $9,095

70. Self-employment tax applies to which of the following activities?

A. Individuals who report only interest and dividend income.
B. A Corporation that reports more than $50,000 in taxable income.
C. Independent contractors reporting net earnings from self-employment of $400 or more.
D. Notary fees totaling $600 or more.

71. Which of the following types of income would be subject to self-employment tax?

A. Notary fees.
B. Income earned by a qualified fisherman.
C. Gains on the sale of a collectible.
D. Punitive damages from a lawsuit.

72. Direct Sellers must report all the income they receive on which Form or Schedule?

A. Schedule E.
B. Schedule SE.
C. Form 1040 line 1.
D. Schedule C.

73. On January 14, 2021, Fuller Engineering, Inc. offers a job to an engineer named Alfred. The position is in another state. Fuller Engineering offers to reimburse Alfred for any moving expenses incurred due to the move. Alfred accepts the job and submits a reimbursement claim for $5,350 for the cost of his move on February 1, 2021. How should this reimbursement be treated by Fuller Engineering, in order to be deductible as a business expense?

A. Moving expense reimbursements are not allowed.
B. The reimbursement is tax-exempt because it is a qualified moving expense.
C. The amounts paid to Alfred must be treated as wages and included on Alfred's Form W-2.
D. The expense is nontaxable to Alfred, but nondeductible to Fuller Engineering.

74. At what level do the at-risk rules apply to an S corporation?

A. Shareholder level.
B. Corporate level.
C. Both shareholder and corporate level.
D. The at-risk rules do not apply.

75. Which of the following would generate passive activity income?

A. A partnership interest in which the partner does not materially participate.
B. The rental activity of a motel owner who materially participates.
C. Social Security Retirement income.
D. Royalties earned by a self-employed writer.

76. All of the following types of lawsuit settlements are taxable *except*:

A. Unlawful discrimination award.
B. Punitive damages awarded in a physical injury-related lawsuit.
C. Settlements for loss in value of property less than the property adjusted basis.
D. Interest paid on a settlement award.

77. Baba-Cola, Inc. owns a factory building with an adjusted basis of $600,000. The company trades the factory building for an office complex with a fair market value of $3,800,000. Baba-Cola pays an additional $270,000 cash to complete the trade. What is Baba-Cola's basis in the office complex and the gain or loss on this transaction?

A. Basis is $600,000; no taxable gain or loss.
B. Basis is $870,000; no taxable gain or loss.
C. Basis is $3,800,000; capital loss of $270,000.
D. Basis is $3,800,000; capital loss of $600,000.

78. The General Business Credit (GBC) is defined as:

A. A set of various credits available to businesses.
B. A single business credit for small businesses.
C. The credit for health insurance provided to employees.
D. A collection of charitable deductions for corporations.

79. Goodie Software, Inc. has 260 employees. The company pays supplemental wages to its employees. Which of the following types of compensation would NOT be included on the employee's Form W-2?

A. Sick leave.
B. Retroactive wage increases.
C. Vacation pay.
D. Worker's compensation.

80. Express Solutions, Inc. is a C Corporation. Express Solutions Inc. pays the personal expenses of an employee-shareholder, Norman, who is also the company president. Express Solutions pays the rent on Norman's apartment and the lease on his personal car. This is an example of a type of a(n):

A. Prohibited transaction.
B. Constructive distribution.
C. Wash sale.
D. Abusive arrangement.

81. Polly is age 39. She is a self-employed wedding planner that reports her income on Schedule C. Polly wants to save for her retirement, and she sets up a SEP-IRA for her business. She does not have any employees. After calculating her income and expenses for the year, she earned $107,000 in net self-employment income. What is the *maximum* amount that Polly can contribute to her SEP-IRA in 2021?

A. $6,000
B. $7,500
C. $26,750
D. $58,000

82. How can an executor elect to transfer the DSUE (Deceased Spousal Unused Exclusion) amount to the surviving spouse?

A. The DSUE is not applicable to estates, only to U.S. trusts.
B. The DSUE is automatic for surviving spouses and no election is necessary.
C. The DSUE election is made on a timely filed Form 706.
D. The DSUE election is made on a timely filed final Form 1040.

83. Hunt Manufacturing, Inc. offers a high deductible health plan (HDHP) to all its employees. The plan is coupled with a Health Savings Account. Hunt Manufacturing sets up an HSA for every qualified employee. Contributions to the employee's HSA may be made by _____.

A. The employee only.
B. The employer only.
C. Only the employee or the employer.
D. By the employee, the employer, or any other person.

84. All of the following statements are correct about the trust fund recovery penalty (TFRP) *except*:

A. The IRS must prove malicious intent for the penalty to be upheld against a non-owner of the company.
B. The IRS can take collection action against the personal assets of anyone deemed a responsible person who willfully failed to pay over the taxes.
C. Trust fund taxes include income tax, Social Security and Medicare taxes that are withheld from employees' wages and held in a trust to be paid to the U.S. Treasury.
D. The amount of the TFRP is equal to the unpaid balance of the trust fund taxes.

85. For most self-employed taxpayers, when is their FIRST estimated tax payment due?

A. January 1.
B. March 1.
C. March 15.
D. April 15.

86. Gracie purchased a van on January 30, 2021, for $24,500 and used it 60% for her mobile notary business. She used it 40% for personal errands. Based on her actual business usage, what is the total *cost* of Gracie's car that qualifies for the section 179 deduction?

A. $0.
B. $9,800.
C. $14,700.
D. $24,500.

87. If an estate's beneficiary sells inherited property that is a capital asset, the gain or loss is considered _____, regardless of how long the beneficiary held the property.

A. Long-term.
B. Short-term.
C. Excludable.
D. Nontaxable.

88. Adella and Gerardo come together to form the Coventry Partnership, LLP. They agree to share profits and losses 50/50. Adella contributed $47,000 in cash to the partnership, and Gerardo contributed depreciable machinery with a fair market value of $98,000 and an adjusted basis of $40,000. What is the Coventry Partnership's basis for depreciation in the contributed machinery?

A. $0
B. $40,000
C. $50,000
D. $98,000

89. Family Focus Charities is a 501(c)(3) exempt entity that is organized as a C corporation. Which form should be used to request an extension of time to file?

A. Form 4868.
B. Form 990-EXT.
C. Form 7004.
D. Form 8868.

90. Which of the following answers properly describes an excise tax?

A. Excise taxes are independent of income taxes.
B. Excise taxes are only imposed on nonresident aliens.
C. Excise taxes are not collected by the IRS, only individual states.
D. Excise taxes are only paid by individuals, estates, and trusts.

91. A paycheck issued after the date of death to a taxpayer for work performed prior to death is considered what type of income?

A. Inheritance income.
B. Income in respect of a decedent.
C. Investment income.
D. Trust income.

92. Mega-Wealth Financial Advisory, Inc. is a cash-basis C Corporation that offers investment services to the general public. Mega-Wealth incurs several casualty losses during the year. Which of the following losses would *not* be deductible as a casualty loss on the business' tax return?

A. Decline in market value of company stock due to accounting fraud.
B. Vandalism done on the exterior of their office building.
C. Fire on the main office building.
D. Embezzlement by a former company officer.

93. Which of the following types of income would NOT be included on Form 941, *Employer's Quarterly Federal Tax Return?*

A. Additional Medicare Tax withheld from employees' pay.
B. The employee's share of Social Security and Medicare taxes.
C. Backup withholding on an employee's pension.
D. Federal income tax withheld from regular wages.

94. Gregory is the sole member of Cobby Coins, LLC. Gregory is a professional dealer of collectible coins and precious metals. A customer purchases 15 gold coins from Gregory for $13,200. The customer pays for the coins with $6,200 in cash, and the rest with a cashier's check of $7,000. What reporting obligation does Gregory have with regards to this transaction? Choose the best answer.

A. Gregory must report the sale on his Schedule C. No other reporting is necessary.
B. Gregory must file an FBAR to report the sale of the gold coins.
C. Gregory must declare the sale on Schedule D.
D. Gregory must file Form 8300 to report this transaction no later than 15 days after the transaction occurred.

95. Peachtree Farms purchased a parcel of farmland during the year. How long should the business retain records relating to the purchase of the land?

A. For three years from the date of purchase.
B. For six years from the date of purchase.
C. Until the statute of limitations expires for the year in which the farm disposes of the property.
D. At least two years after the year in which the business disposes of the property.

96. Aaron is a self-employed rancher who files on Schedule F. How would he calculate his self-employment (SE) tax for the year?

A. Aaron would calculate his SE tax on page 1 of Form 1040.
B. Aaron would calculate his SE tax directly on Schedule F.
C. Aaron would calculate his SE tax on Schedule SE and attach it to his Form 1040.
D. Qualified farmers and fishermen do not pay self-employment tax on their earnings.

97. Which of the following employers are not required to file a Form 941 on a quarterly basis?

A. Employers of farm employees.
B. Exempt entities with employees.
C. Governmental entities.
D. Sole-proprietors with fewer than five employees.

98. A closely-held corporation can qualify as a "real estate professional" if more than _____ of the gross receipts for its tax year came from real property trades or businesses in which it materially participated.

A. 40%
B. 50%
C. 80%
D. 90%

99. When a business is sold through an asset sale, how is the sale generally treated for tax purposes?

A. The sale of the business is usually treated as the sale of a single asset.
B. Each business asset is treated as being sold separately for determining the overall gain or loss.
C. Each asset's basis is re-calculated in accordance with Federal Regulations.
D. Each asset is considered in aggregate, resulting in a long-term or short-term capital gain or loss.

100. Which of the following actions would potentially enable a business to claim the Work Opportunity Tax Credit?

A. A corporation that hires an ex-felon.
B. A corporation that manufactures U.S. goods.
C. A partnership that invests in U.S. savings bonds.
D. A sole proprietorship that builds houses for impoverished neighborhoods.

Please review your answer choices with the correct answers in the next section.

Answers to Exam #2: Businesses

1. The answer is D. The Tax Cuts and Jobs Act eliminated the deduction for *most* business-related entertainment expenses, so the tickets to the golf tournament are not deductible, even if the entertainment activity was related to a client. In 2021, business-related meals provided in a restaurant are 100% deductible. Team-building activities, like employee holiday parties, are still 100% deductible if the expense is "primarily for the benefit of employees who are not highly compensated or key employees." This would include things like a company picnic or an office party. The snacks in the breakroom would be subject to the 50% meal limit. The answer is calculated as follows:

Expense	Cost	Allowable?	Amount
Tickets to a golfing tournament with a corporate client	$240	NO	$0
Business meals at restaurants	152	100% deductible	152
Snacks and beverages for the employee break room (bought for the office)	260	50% deductible	130
Office party for Teddy's employees and their families	552	100% deductible	552
Allowable deduction on Schedule C			**$834**

2. The answer is C. Phillip's basis in the new property is $244,000 (this is figured by adding his original $50,000 adjusted basis in the *old* property (the residential rental) plus the $194,000 additional cash he paid during the exchange). His basis in the farmland is $244,000 unless he has any other increases or decreases to his original basis (question modified from an example in IRS Publication 463).

3. The answer is D. Benicio is a **statutory employee**. A statutory employee is an independent contractor (who files on Schedule C) but is treated as an employee for FICA tax purposes. A statutory employee is classified as one of the following:

- A driver who distributes beverages (other than milk) or meat, vegetables, fruit, or bakery products; or who picks up and delivers laundry or dry cleaning if the driver is an agent or is paid on commission.
- A full-time life insurance sales agent whose principal business activity is selling life insurance or annuity contracts, or both, primarily for one life insurance company.
- An individual who works at home on materials or goods that you supply and that must be returned to the business.
- A full-time traveling or city salesperson who works on a business' behalf and turns in orders from wholesalers, retailers, contractors, or operators of hotels, restaurants, or other similar establishments. The goods sold must be merchandise for resale or supplies for use in the buyer's business operation.

If a person is a statutory employee, "statutory employee" in box 13 of Form W-2 should be checked.

4. The answer is A. The 199A QBI deduction permits owners of eligible businesses to deduct up to 20% of their qualified business income from taxable income. However, if the business is a "specified service business," the deduction is phased out based on the owner's pre-QBI deduction taxable income and potentially based on the amount of wages and qualifying property of the business. For the purposes of the Section 199A tax deduction, a "Specified Service Trade or Business" (SSTB) would include:

- Health services (including doctors, dentists, physical therapists, and veterinarians),
- Legal services (lawyers, mediators, and paralegals),
- Accounting (CPA firms, tax preparation firms, and bookkeepers),
- Actuarial science,
- Performing arts (including musicians, entertainers, actors, and singers),
- Consulting (includes professional advisors and lobbyists),
- Athletics (including athletes, team managers, and coaches),
- Financial services (including financial advisors, investment bankers, wealth planners, and retirement advisors),
- Brokerage services (including stock brokers or any other professional where a person arranges transactions between a buyer and a seller with respect to securities for a commission or a fee) or;
- Endorsement of products or services.

Engineering and architectural services were initially included in this list when the TCJA was originally introduced and was pending legislation, but Congress removed those fields in the final version of the TCJA. Real estate brokers, hotel/motel operators, property managers, and bankers are also excluded from the definition of a "Specified Service Business."

5. The answer is B. Tax shelters (regardless of their size) are always required to use the accrual method of accounting, rather than the cash method. All the other entities listed would be permitted to use the cash method of accounting. Most businesses with less than $26 million in average annual gross receipts over the prior three tax years, for 2021, can use the cash method of accounting.

6. The answer is D. Dewey cannot deduct contributions to an HSA on his Schedule C. A health savings account (HSA) is a tax-favored medical savings account available to taxpayers. Contributions to an HSA are deductible, but not as a business expense. For individual taxpayers, contributions to an HSA are only deductible as an adjustment to income. Taxpayers must be covered by a high-deductible health plan (HDHP) to be able to take advantage of an HSA.

7. The answer is B. An S corporation has similarities to both a C corporation and a partnership. Like a partnership, an S corporation is a pass-through entity and is generally not taxed on its earnings. Instead, income and losses pass through to shareholders. Like a C corporation, an S corporation enjoys liability protection that a partnership does not. However, S corporations are less flexible than partnerships, and there are some instances in which an S corporation is forced to pay tax on some of its earnings. Although uncommon, there are some corporate-level taxes that may apply to S corporations in certain situations (such as the *built-in gains* tax). There are also restrictions on the number and types of shareholders an S corporation can have.

8. The answer is C. Lorex Chemicals' basis in the property at the time of the sale was $932,000 ($940,000 cost + $40,000 improvements – $48,000 depreciation). The company received net proceeds of $2,746,000 ($2,000,000 + $400,000 + $340,000 + $6,000), resulting in a recognized gain of **$1,814,000**.

> **Note:** This is not a qualifying Section 1031 exchange, even though Lorex Chemicals purchased another building shortly thereafter. This is because the original transaction was a cash sale. There was no actual "exchange" of "like-kind" properties, and the business did not use a qualified intermediary to facilitate the exchange, which would be required in a deferred exchange.

9. The answer is D. Willard's single-owner LLC will automatically be classified as a "disregarded" entity, or not separate, from its owner for income tax purposes, **unless** the owner files Form 8832, *Entity Classification Election*, and chooses to be taxed as a C corporation, or a Form 2553 to be taxed as an S Corporation. Thus, a single-owner LLC owned by an individual is treated as a sole proprietorship, and the owner is subject to the tax on net earnings from self-employment. Similarly, a single-owner LLC owned by a corporation or a partnership is included in the owner's tax return as if it were a division of the corporation or partnership.

10. The answer is B. There is no such thing as the "cost-price method." All of the other choices are valid methods for accounting for inventory.

11. The answer is A. A tax-exempt organization cannot be classified as a partnership. Certain entities with different legal structures may be classified as partnerships for tax purposes, either based upon their election by filing Form 8832, *Entity Classification Election*, or by default (as in the case of a domestic LLC with at least two members that is classified as a partnership unless it files Form 8832 and elects to be treated as a corporation). However, the following organizations are prohibited from being classified as partnerships for tax purposes:
- A corporation (although a corporation can be a "partner" in a partnership).
- A joint-stock company or joint-stock association.
- An insurance company.
- Certain banks.
- A government entity.
- An organization required to be taxed as a corporation by the IRS.
- Certain foreign organizations.
- Any tax-exempt (non-profit) organization.
- Any real estate investment trust (REIT).
- Any organization classified as a trust or estate.
- Any other organization that elects to be classified as a corporation by filing Form 8832.

12. The answer is D. Amounts reimbursed under an accountable plan are generally not taxable and are therefore exempt from FICA. Wages include (but are not limited to) the following:
- Salaries, hourly pay, contingent fees, piece rate, or payments by the job.
- Commissions and bonuses.
- Vacation pay, severance pay, sick pay, and strike benefits.
- The reasonable cash value of compensation paid in property (other than cash).

13. The answer is A. To be deductible, a business expense must be both "ordinary" and "necessary." An *ordinary* expense is one that is common and accepted in the taxpayer's field of business. A *necessary* expense is one that is helpful and appropriate for the business.

14. The answer is C. Any business (including a corporation) adopts its tax year and its accounting method when it files its first income tax return.

15. The answer is A. Nestor can take a depreciation deduction of $1,000 [($10,000 distribution ÷ $30,000) × $3,000], and Bradley can take a deduction of $2,000 [($20,000 distribution ÷ $30,000) × $3,000]. Just like individuals, trusts and estates can have income from a trade or business, even after the original owner of the business has died. The allowable deductions for depreciation and depletion that accrue after the decedent's death must be apportioned between the estate and the beneficiaries, depending on the income of the estate allocable to each. In this case, the depreciation deduction would be allocatable ratably to Jane's beneficiaries based on the income that is apportioned to each of her sons (question based on an example from Publication 559).

16. The answer is B. The federal government levies an excise tax on various motor fuels. Excise taxes may be deductible currently or as the item is used, or may be subject to capitalization. Excise taxes are often paid when purchases are made on a specific item, such as gasoline, or activity, such as highway usage by trucks. When paid in connection with the purchase of a particular item, an excise tax is considered part of the cost of that item. Therefore, it may be deductible currently or as the item is used, or be subject to capitalization, such as when the item is used in manufacturing inventory. When a business collects excise taxes, it serves solely as a collection agent for the government, and the amounts collected are passed through without any effects on business revenue or profits.

17. The answer is C. The mileage reimbursements are not taxable to Michelle and do not have to be reported on her Form W-2. Mileage reimbursements made to an employee under an accountable plan are not included on an employee's Form W-2. These are amounts that are not taxable to the employee and not reportable as wages. An accountable plan is a formal or written arrangement whereby an employer reimburses an employee for business expenses. The employee provides documentation of the expense, and the employer is allowed to deduct the expenses as normal business expenses. The employee does not have to recognize the reimbursements as income.

18. The answer is D. Bobby and Sienna cannot set up a joint HSA. Spouses cannot have a joint HSA. Each spouse who is an eligible individual must open a separate HSA. This is regardless of whether or not the spouses file jointly or separately.

19. The answer is B. Sales tax collected by a business is a liability, not income, in a state where sales tax is imposed on the *buyer*, and the seller is merely collecting the sales tax as an agent of the state. The business must remit those sales taxes to the government. As a result, collected sales tax falls under the liability category on the balance sheet (question based on an EA exam question released by Prometric).

> **Note:** In some states, the sales tax is imposed on the *seller*. In these situations, any sales taxes collected from the buyer would be included in the business' gross income.

20. The answer is D. A tax-exempt organization may be subject to UBIT. Although an exempt organization must be operated primarily for tax-exempt purposes, it may engage in income-producing activities that are unrelated to those purposes, as long as these activities are not a substantial part of the organization's regular activities. Income from unrelated business activities is subject to a federal tax called the unrelated business income tax (UBIT). For most organizations, an activity is considered an unrelated business and subject to UBIT if:

- It is a trade or business,
- It is regularly carried on, and
- It is not substantially related to furthering the exempt purpose of the organization.

21. The answer is B. The TCJA set a flat tax of 21% on C corporations. This was a permanent change. The corporate tax rate also applies to LLCs or other eligible business entities who have elected to be taxed as Corporations. The TCJA also permanently eliminated the corporate alternative minimum tax (AMT).

22. The answer is A. Wages paid to an employee of a partnership are not a partnership distribution; the wages would merely be treated as a business expense. Partnership distributions include the following.

- A withdrawal by a partner in anticipation of the current year's earnings.
- A distribution of the current year's or prior years' earnings not needed for working capital.
- A complete or partial liquidation of a partner's interest.
- A distribution to all partners in a complete liquidation of the partnership.

23. The answer is C. Econix Corporation's basis in the land and building is $650,000. The contributing shareholder's basis in the property was $450,000, and any gain that is recognized by Logan must be added to the corporation's basis. Since Logan received cash in this transaction, he has to calculate gain. Logan's recognized gain is the lesser of: (1) his realized gain or (2) the boot received in the transaction. Logan's realized gain is $250,000 ($700,000 FMV - $450,000 basis). The boot he received was $200,000 in cash. Therefore, the gain recognized by Logan is $200,000, and the corporation's basis in the property is $650,000 ($450,000 carryover basis + the $200,000 income recognized by Logan).

24. The answer is D. Carey may postpone recognizing the income from crop insurance payments if he uses the cash method. Crop insurance proceeds and government disaster payments are generally taxable in the year they are received. However, a farmer can elect to postpone reporting the income until the following year if he meets the following conditions:

- The farming business must use the *cash method* of accounting.
- Crop insurance proceeds were received in the same tax year the crops were damaged.
- Under normal business practices, the farming business would have reported income from the damaged crops in any tax year following the year the damage occurred.

25. The answer is B. If Karen wants her LLC to be classified as an S corporation, she must file Form 2553, *Election by a Small Business Corporation*. This form is used instead of Form 8832 when an LLC makes the election to be taxed as an S corporation. Form 2553 must be signed and dated by a corporate officer. If Form 2553 isn't signed, it won't be considered timely-filed.

26. The answer is B. Boggle Corporation's basis in the newly acquired real property is $380,000 (the $300,000 adjusted basis of the old parcel plus the $80,000 paid). The fair market value of either property is irrelevant in the basis calculation. The answer is calculated as follows:

Cost of old office complex	$500,000
Subtract depreciation on old office building	-200,000
Adjusted basis of old office building	$300,000
Add cash paid for new property	+$80,000
Adjusted basis of factory building	**$380,000**

In a 1031 exchange, if a business trades property and also pays money, the basis of the property received is the basis of the property given up, increased by any additional money paid (question based on an example in Publication 551, under Nontaxable Exchanges).

27. The answer is D. The destruction of the taxpayer's tractor is a section 1033 involuntary conversion. Travis has until December 31, 2023 (two years) to reinvest the insurance proceeds in a new tractor or other qualifying replacement property. The replacement period generally ends two years *after the close* of the first tax year in which the taxpayer realizes gain from the involuntary conversion. Travis is not required to report the insurance proceeds on his tax return unless he fails to reinvest the proceeds in qualifying replacement property (such as a new tractor).

28. The answer is A. A corporation that does not file its tax return by the due date, including extensions, may be penalized 5% of the unpaid tax for each month or part of a month the return is late, up to a maximum of **25%** of the unpaid tax.

29. The answer is D. A general partner in a partnership is considered to be self-employed. Partners are not considered employees and should not be issued a Form W-2. Instead, they are issued a Schedule K-1, and each partner includes his share of the partnership's income on his individual tax return.

30. The answer is C. Sutton's driving expenses are equal to 56¢ x 2,600 = $1,456. The business meals at restaurants are 100% deductible in 2021. The baseball tickets are entertainment, and therefore not deductible. The answer is figured as follows:

Expense	Amount	Allowable?	Amount
Supply expenses	$17,750	100% deductible	$17,750
Business meals	$400	100% deductible	$400
Entertainment (baseball game)	$350	Not deductible	$0
Mileage (56¢ per mile is the 2021 rate)	2,600 x 56¢	100% deductible	$1,456
Allowable deduction on Schedule C			**$19,606**

31. The answer is D. The IRS evaluates three primary characteristics to determine the relationship between a business and workers it pays for services:

- *Behavioral Control:* Covers whether the business has a right to direct or control how the work is done.
- *Financial Control:* Covers whether the business has a right to direct or control the financial and business aspects of the worker's job.
- *Type of Relationship:* Relates to how the worker and the business owner perceive their relationship.

Whether a person is classified as an employee or an independent contractor depends on the facts and circumstances of each individual case. Employers who misclassify workers as independent contractors may face substantial tax penalties for failing to pay employment taxes and failing to file payroll tax forms.

32. The answer is A. Donna must recognize ordinary income of $15,000 as payment for services she rendered to the corporation. If a taxpayer transfers property (or money and property) to a corporation in exchange for stock in that corporation, and immediately afterwards is in control of the corporation, the exchange is usually not taxable under IRC section 351. To be "in control" of a corporation, the transferor must own, immediately after the transfer, at least 80% of the total combined voting power of all classes of stock. However, this nonrecognition treatment does not include services rendered to the issuing corporation. The value of stock received for services is income to the recipient.

33. The answer is B. Chateau Winery, Inc. does not have to wait until it files its tax return to request a refund of its overpaid estimated tax. The business can file Form 4466, *Corporation Application for Quick Refund of Overpayment of Estimated Tax.* A corporation that has overpaid its estimated tax may apply for a quick refund if the overpayment is at least 10% of its expected income tax liability and at least $500.

34. The answer is A. Pauly is required to subtract the cost of personal use items from total purchases if he removes items for personal-use from business inventory. Goods that are withdrawn from the business and taken by the owner would reduce the inventory of the business. It is not treated as an expense of the business (see IRS Publication 334, *Tax Guide for Small Business*, for more information).

35. The answer is C. Qualified creative expenses incurred as a freelance (self-employed) writer, photographer, or artist are not subject to the Uniform Capitalization Rules, regardless of the business' gross receipts threshold. A business must use the uniform capitalization rules if it:

- Produces (or manufactures) real or tangible personal property for use in the business or activity.
- Produces (or manufactures) real or tangible personal property for sale to customers.
- Acquires property (inventory) for resale.

For the purposes of this rule, "tangible personal property" includes films, sound recordings, videotapes, books, or similar property (see IRS Publication 551, Basis of Assets, for more information).

36. The answer is D. The annual accounting period for your income tax return is called a *tax year.* A business can use one of the following tax years:

- A calendar tax year.
- A fiscal tax year.

See IRS Publication 334, *Tax Guide for Small Businesses,* for more information on accounting periods.

37. The answer is D. The cost of advertising is a deductible expense. It is not included in the cost of goods sold. The following expenses are examples of costs that are included in a business' cost of goods sold:

- The cost of products or raw materials (including freight-in).
- Storage costs for inventory.
- Direct labor costs.
- Factory overhead.

Only the direct costs related to the production of inventory are generally included in COGS. Other costs, such as shipping of finished products and advertising, are not included in COGS and are simply deducted as a business expense. For additional information, refer to the chapter on Cost of Goods Sold, Publication 334, *Tax Guide for Small Businesses,* and the chapter on Inventories, Publication 538, *Accounting Periods and Methods.*

38. The answer is C. Danika is most likely a *"statutory nonemployee."* There are two main categories of statutory non-employees: direct sellers and licensed real estate agents. They are treated as self-employed for federal tax purposes, including income and employment taxes, if:

- Payments for their services are directly related to sales rather than to the number of hours worked, and
- Services are performed under a written contract providing that they will not be treated as employees for federal tax purposes.

Compensation for a statutory non-employee is reported on Form 1099-NEC. Danika would report her income and loss on Schedule C.

39. The answer is A. A company that accumulates $100,000 or more in taxes on *any day* during a monthly or semi-weekly deposit period is required to deposit the tax by the next business day. This schedule supersedes the normal semi-weekly or monthly payroll deposit requirements.

40. The answer is A. When a business files its first tax return, it can choose any permitted accounting method. Subsequent changes, either in the overall accounting method or the treatment of a material item, generally require that the taxpayer obtain IRS approval. Prior approval is required for:

- Changes from cash to accrual or vice versa, unless the change is required by tax law.
- Changes in the method used to value inventory, such as switching from LIFO to FIFO.
- Changes in the method of depreciation or amortization.

The taxpayer must file Form 3115, *Application for Change in Accounting Method*, to request a change in either an overall accounting method or the accounting treatment for an individual item. However, IRS consent is not required for the following:

- Making an adjustment in the useful life of a depreciable or amortizable asset (but a taxpayer cannot change the recovery period for MACRS or ACRS property).
- Correcting a math error or an error in figuring tax liability.
- A change in accounting method when the change is required by tax law.

A business does not need prior IRS approval to change its name. Business owners can simply submit a name change for their business.

41. The answer is B. The short-term gain offsets some of the long-term loss, leaving a net capital loss of $8,000. Windsor Windows, Inc. must treat this $8,000 loss as a *short-term* loss when carried back or carried forward. The capital losses cannot be claimed against ordinary corporate income.

> **Note:** C corporations must generally carryback a net capital loss three years and carryforward up to a maximum of five years. The carryback (for almost all situations) is *mandatory* (IRC Section 1212(a)(1)). If any capital loss carryforward remains after carrying the loss forward for five years, it is lost.

42. The answer is B. An S corporation cannot have more than 100 shareholders (certain related family members count as a single shareholder for purposes of the 100-shareholder limit). Shareholders must *generally* be U.S. citizens or U.S. residents; however, there is an exception for certain tax-exempt organizations and certain trusts and estates.

43. The answer is A. No loss is allowed in this scenario. Although the Concrete Partnership realized a $35,000 loss on the sale of the cement mixer, because the partnerships are considered "related parties" (a single person owns more than 50% of capital and profits in both entities), the losses are not deductible. Only when the property is later sold to an *unrelated* party, the suspended losses then would be available to reduce any realized gains.

44. The answer is D. A C corporation generally does not have to use a required tax year and can use any fiscal year instead. An exception exists for a C corporation that is a Personal Service Corporation, which generally must use a calendar year. Partnerships, S corporations, and sole proprietorships generally must use a "required tax year," which is a tax year required under the Internal Revenue Code. The two basic choices for a required tax year are: a calendar year or a fiscal year. An entity does not have to use a "required tax year" if it receives permission from the IRS to use another tax year, establishes a *bona fide* business purpose for using a fiscal year, or if it files an election under section 444. A business adopts a tax year when it files its first income tax return. In the case of a sole proprietorship, for example, the "required tax year" would be a calendar year, because it coincides with the individual owner's tax year.

45. The answer is B. A partnership interest is not a section 197 asset. Section 197 assets are intangible assets used in a trade or business. Section 197 assets include: goodwill, going concern value, workforce in place, patents, copyrights, franchises, trademarks, and trade names.

46. The answer is C. The IRS advises employers to keep all employment tax records for at least four years. These records should be available for IRS review (see Publication 583, *Starting a Business and Keeping Records*).

47. The answer is D. Since Sachs Group, Inc. has *qualifying financial statements*, it can deduct items that cost up to $5,000 per invoice or per item under the *de minimis safe harbor* of the final tangible property regulations. A written accounting policy is *required* for taxpayers with an applicable financial statement. "Applicable financial statements" include financial statements required to be filed with the Securities and Exchange Commission (SEC), other federal or state agencies, as well as other types of certified audited financial statements accompanied by an official CPA report. A taxpayer that does *not* have qualifying financial statements can deduct items that cost up to $2,500 per invoice or item under the *de minimis safe harbor*.

48. The answer is A. Taxable income will increase an S corporation shareholder's basis. Unlike a C corporation, each year, a shareholder's stock basis of an S corporation increases or decreases based upon the S corporation's operations. In general, an income item will *increase* stock basis while a loss, deduction, or distribution will *decrease* a shareholder's stock basis.

49. The answer is C. The Paskins Partnership cannot elect out of the centralized partnership audit regime (CPAR), because the partnership has a partner that is a grantor trust. Only eligible partnerships can elect out of the CPAR, and only on a timely filed tax return (Form 1065). An "eligible" partnership:

- Must have 100 or fewer partners during the year, and
- Has only "eligible partners" which include:
    - Individuals (natural persons **only**, not LLCs, and not grantor trusts!)
    - C Corporations or foreign entities classified as corporations
    - S corporations
    - Estates of deceased partners (but not bankruptcy estates!)

Partnerships with non-qualified partners cannot opt-out of the centralized audit regime, even if the partnership has fewer than 100 partners.

50. The answer is D. The computation of recapture amounts is not necessary when the business use percentage of section 179 or listed property exceeds 50% (for more information, see IRS *Instructions for Form 4797*).

51. The answer is D. In 2021, McCarthy Accountancy, Inc. may deduct 100% of the meal per diem amounts on its tax return as a business expense.[15] Amounts paid for meals under the federal *per diem* rate are deductible by the employer. The amounts are not taxable wages and are not subject to income tax withholding or payment of Social Security, Medicare, and FUTA taxes. "Per diem" is an allowance paid to employees for lodging, meals, and incidental expenses incurred when traveling on behalf of a business. This allowance is in lieu of paying their actual travel expenses. IRS Publication 1542, *Per Diem Rates*, provides the rates for all continental U.S. areas.

> **Note:** The Consolidated Appropriations Act of 2020 (CAA) allows a full 100% deduction for "food or beverages provided by a restaurant." The IRS issued Notice 2021-25 that the 100% deduction also applies to per diem meals. This would **not** include meals purchased at an establishment that primarily sells prepackaged foods, which means that grocery stores, convenience stores, gas stations, would not qualify. Those meals would be subject to the 50% limit for most businesses.

52. The answer is A. An exempt organization may qualify under Section 501(c)(3) if it is organized exclusively for charitable, religious, educational, testing for public safety, fostering amateur sports competition, or preventing cruelty to children or animals. The other organizations listed may qualify as tax-exempt organizations if certain rules are met, but they would not qualify as charitable organizations under Section 501(c)(3).

---

[15] On November 16, 2021 the Internal Revenue Service issued Notice 2021-63, clarifying that the 100% deduction allowable as a meal expense in 2021 for meals provided by a restaurant also applies to the meal portion of a per diem rate or allowance.

53. The answer is D. In general, a "fiscal tax year" is 12 consecutive months ending on the last day of any month *except* December.

54. The answer is C. Bargain Retail would be considered an Applicable Large Employer under the ACA. An Applicable Large Employer is any business that has an average of at least 50 full-time employees or "full-time equivalents." For the purposes of the Affordable Care Act, a full-time employee is someone who works at least 30 hours a week. In the question, the company's 20 part-time employees would be counted as 10 full-time employees working 40 hours per week, or 10 "full-time equivalents." Forty full-time employees plus an additional 10 "full-time equivalents" would equal 50 full-time employees, making Bargain Retail an Applicable Large Employer for tax purposes under the Affordable Care Act.[16]

55. The answer is B. A below-market loan is a loan on which no interest is charged or on which interest is charged at a rate below the applicable federal rate (AFR). If a corporation makes a below-market loan to one of its shareholders, the corporation generally is deemed to make a payment to the shareholder. If the shareholder is not an employee, the imputed amount is usually treated as a dividend.[17]

56. The answer is C. After the death of a taxpayer, if an individual beneficiary receives IRD and includes it on their return, they *are* allowed to claim a deduction for the estate tax paid on that income if Form 706 was filed. Income that the decedent had a right to receive is included in the decedent's gross estate and is subject to estate tax. This "income in respect of a decedent" is also taxed when received by the recipient (estate or beneficiary). However, an income tax deduction is allowed to the recipient for the estate tax paid on the income.[18]

57. The answer is D. Hillenbrand Foods, Inc. has until **April 18, 2022,** (the due date of their 2021 return) to make the contribution. An accrual-based C corporation is allowed to deduct charitable contributions authorized during the taxable year by the board of directors and paid *by the due date* for filing the corporation's tax return (not including extensions). In 2021, C corporations can deduct cash contributions up to 25% of taxable income (calculated before any charitable contribution deduction, NOL carryback, capital loss carryback, or dividends received deduction). Since the corporation's taxable income was $105,000 (before any charitable contribution deduction), only 25% of this amount (or **$26,250**) is deductible on the corporation's tax return. Hillenbrand Foods Inc. must make the contribution no later than the unextended due date of its tax return.[19]

> **Note:** April 18, 2022 is the deadline for 2021 corporate tax returns due to the Emancipation Day holiday in Washington DC.

---

[16] Note that only the ACA penalty for individuals was repealed by the Tax Cuts and Jobs Act. The ACA provisions for large employers remain in full force.

[17] For more information, see IRC Section 7872(c), IRC, §7872, and Publication 535.

[18] This question is based on an actual exam question released by the IRS. See IRC §691 and Publication 559, *Survivors, Executors and Administrators.*

[19] The CARES Act temporarily increased the AGI limit for charitable gifts for corporate taxpayers. A corporation can claim a deduction up to 25% of the corporation's taxable income for cash charitable gifts made in 2021. The 25% limit also applies to donations of food inventory. All other types of donations are limited to 10% of corporate taxable income. This rule only applies to C Corporations.

58. The answer is B. Christopher qualifies for the QBI deduction because he is a statutory employee. Generally, wages are not considered QBI, but performance of services as a statutory employee are considered QBI and are eligible for the QBI deduction to the extent that all other requirements of Section 199A are satisfied.[20]

59. The answer is C. Depreciation is an allowable business expense on Schedule F and Schedule C. The other deductions listed are allowed only as adjustments to income on Schedule 1 of Form 1040.

60. The answer is B. The standard mileage rate in 2021 is 56¢ a mile. Edmund can take a mileage deduction of $8,960 (16,000 miles × 56¢). The parking fees and tolls are also deductible, but they would be deducted separately. Edmund may also deduct any other ordinary and necessary business expenses, such as supplies, a cell phone, food and drinks for passengers, parking fees, tolls, roadside assistance plans, business insurance, and taxes (question modified directly from an example in Publication 4491).

61. The answer is B. Calvin may deduct $140 for business-related gifts on his Schedule C. The answer is calculated as follows: $25 for client #1 + $25 for client #2 + $25 for client #3 + $65 packaging/shipping = $140. A business can deduct business-related gifts to clients and customers, but the deductible amount is limited to $25 for amounts given to any person during the year. However, the $25 limit for business gifts does not include incidental costs, such as packaging, insurance, and mailing costs, or the cost of engraving jewelry, which can be deducted separately.

62. The answer is D. The deadline to file Form 5500, *Annual Return/Report of Employee Benefit Plan,* is the last day of the seventh month after the end of the plan year. So, for example, a calendar-year retirement plan would be required to file on July 31.

63. The answer is D. For James to deduct his business miles as an expense, he is required to maintain a detailed mileage log. The mileage log must include a record of:
- The taxpayer's business mileage.
- The dates of their business trips.
- The places the taxpayer drove for business, and,
- The business purpose of the trips.

64. The answer is C. Goodwill and going-concern are both section 197 intangible assets that must be amortized over 15 years (180 months).

65. The answer is B. Port Express Inc. does have to obtain IRS consent to correct a depreciation error based on the use of an incorrect class life of an asset. However, for this type of change, going from an impermissible method of accounting for depreciation (having depreciated the ferry over an incorrect class life for multiple years) to a permissible method, under Revenue Procedure 2019-43 this will be handled through the automatic IRS consent procedures. The company will file Form 3115 and claim the section 481(a) adjustment to correct the error. The business should not file amended returns to correct the error.

---

[20] Payments made to statutory employees, as defined in section 3121(d)(3), are excluded from the definition of wages considered income from the trade or business of performing services as an employee under Treasury Regulation section 1.199A-5(d)(1).

66. The answer is B. Federal income taxes are never deductible as a business expense by any type of entity. Penalties assessed on delinquent federal income taxes are also never deductible.

67. The answer is C. The age of a worker would not be a factor in determining worker classification. Facts that provide evidence of the degree of control and independence fall into three categories:

- Behavioral control: Does the company control or have the right to control what the worker does and how the worker does his or her job?
- Financial control: Are the business aspects of the worker's job controlled by the payer? (these include things like how a worker is paid, whether expenses are reimbursed, who provides tools/supplies, etc.)
- Relationship of the Parties: Are there written contracts or employee type benefits (i.e., pension plan, insurance, vacation pay, etc.)? Will the relationship continue and is the work performed a key aspect of the business?

Additional information about worker classification are in Publication 1779, Independent Contractor or Employee, and Publication 1976, Independent Contractor or Employee; Section 530 Employment Tax Relief Requirements.

68. The answer is D. All of the costs are deductible under section 179 on Bonnie's business return, so her allowable deduction would be $19,750 ($4,500 + $12,000 +$3,250). In the past, the section 179 deduction was generally not allowed for property used in connection with rental activity. However, the TCJA expanded the definition of eligible property to include depreciable tangible property used predominantly to "furnish lodging."[21] This would include something like a hotel, motel, dormitory or a hostel (but it would not include regular residential rentals).

69. The answer is B. Josephine's total travel expenses would be figured as follows:

([8,000 miles × 56¢ per mile = $4,480] + $250 for parking and tolls = **$4,730**

Josephine's total deduction for transportation expenses on Schedule C would be $4,730. In 2021, the standard mileage rate for the cost of operating a car, van, or truck for each mile of business use is 56¢ per mile.

> **Note:** The volunteering miles would also be potentially deductible, but only as a charitable deduction on Schedule A. Make sure you read the questions carefully because the EA exam will often include scenarios like this. Automobile expenses (or mileage) incurred while volunteering for charitable organizations *are* deductible, but never as a business expense on Schedule C.

70. The answer is C. A taxpayer generally must pay self-employment tax if they have net earnings from self-employment of $400 or more. Answer "A" is incorrect because interest and dividends are not subject to self-employment tax. Answer "B" is incorrect because corporations are subject to a flat income tax of 21%. Self-employment tax only applies to individual taxpayers. Answer "D" is incorrect because notary fees for services provided by a notary public are not subject to self-employment tax.

---

[21] Section 179 property used predominantly to "furnish lodging" generally includes, for example, beds and other furniture, refrigerators, ranges, and other equipment used in the living quarters of a lodging facility such as an apartment house, hotel, dormitory, or any other facility where sleeping accommodations are provided. This definition does not include passive residential rentals where the owner does not materially participate. See Treas. Reg. sec. 1.179-4(a).

71. The answer is B. Income earned by a sole proprietor would be subject to self-employment tax. This includes income by a qualified fisherman. The other choices would be subject to *income* tax, but generally not subject to self-employment tax.

72. The answer is D. Direct sellers of products or services typically must report their income on Schedule C. Direct sellers and licensed real estate agents are treated as statutory nonemployees by statute. They are treated as self-employed for all federal tax purposes, including income and employment taxes (this question is directly modified from a released IRS exam question).

73. The answer is C. The amounts paid to Alfred must be treated as wages and included on Alfred's Form W-2, otherwise, Fuller Engineering will not be able to deduct the expense. The actual reimbursement is allowable, but only if it is treated as taxable compensation (wages). The TCJA suspended the qualified moving expense exclusion and employee deduction for moving expenses. If an employer offers to pay these expenses as a condition of employment, the amounts are treated as taxable compensation and must be reported and treated as wages in order to be deductible to the business. This treatment applies even if the company has an accountable plan.[22]

74. The answer is A. The at-risk rules apply to S corporations at the *shareholder* level. For C corporations, the at-risk rules apply at the corporate level, but only for certain closely-held corporations. The at-risk rules are designed to prevent business owners from claiming losses in excess of their amount of investment at risk in the business activity.

75. The answer is A. There are two kinds of passive activities: (1) trade or business activities in which the taxpayer does not materially participate, and (2) rental activities; *unless* the taxpayer is a real estate professional, or a hotel or motel operator who materially participates in the activity. Answer "D" is incorrect because royalties earned by a self-employed writer would be earned income, not passive income (these taxpayers would report their royalty income on Schedule C, rather than Schedule E). Answer "C" is incorrect because Social Security income is not "passive activity income" by definition - it is *pension* income. For more information, see IRS Publication 925, *Passive Activity and At-Risk Rules.*

76. The answer is C. Settlements for loss in value of property that are *less* than the adjusted basis of a taxpayer's property are not taxable and generally do not need to be reported. A taxpayer must reduce his basis in the property by the amount of the settlement. If the property settlement exceeds the adjusted basis in the property, the excess is taxable income. The taxability of other types of settlements varies. For instance, in employment-related lawsuits such as unlawful discrimination or involuntary termination, the portion of the proceeds that is for lost wages is taxable. *Punitive damages* and interest on settlements also are generally taxable, even if the lawsuit or settlement is related to a physical injury. Settlements for physical injuries or illness are generally not taxable, although the proceeds for emotional distress often are (unless the emotional distress originates from physical injury or illness).

---

[22] There is a narrow exception for active-duty members of the armed forces. U.S. military personnel can still deduct moving expenses and receive non-taxable reimbursement for their moving expenses.

77. The answer is B. This is a qualified like-kind exchange (the exchange of real property), so Baba-Cola has no recognized gain on the transaction as no boot was received and only cash boot was given to the other party. The basis of the new property is equal to the sum of the amount paid ($270,000) plus the adjusted basis of the old property (the factory). The answer is figured as follows: ($600,000 + $270,000 = **$870,000**).

78. The answer is A. The General Business Credit consists of various credits available to businesses. The GBC also may include the total carryforward of business credits from prior years.

79. The answer is D. Worker's compensation is not taxable to the recipient at the state or federal level, and therefore, not included on Form W-2. "Supplemental wages" are compensation paid to an employee in addition to regular wages and include, but are not limited to: bonuses, commissions, overtime pay, sick leave, severance pay, vacation pay, retroactive wage increases, and payments for nondeductible moving expenses.

80. The answer is B. The payments of Norman's personal expenses, regardless of his position in the company, would be treated as a constructive distribution. Certain transactions between a corporation and its shareholders may be regarded as constructive distributions. They may be dividends or nondividend distributions, and may be taxable to the shareholders. Examples include when a corporation:

- Pays personal expenses on behalf of an employee-shareholder.
- Pays an employee-shareholder an unreasonably high salary considering the services actually performed.
- Rents property from a shareholder and the rent is unreasonably higher than the shareholder would charge an unrelated party for the use of the same property.
- Cancels a shareholder's debt without repayment by the shareholder.
- Loans money to a shareholder on an interest-free basis or at a below market rate.

81. The answer is C. Polly can contribute a maximum of $26,750 in 2021. The maximum amount for contribution to a SEP-IRA plan in 2021 is the *lesser* of $58,000 (in 2021) or 25% of the participant's compensation. The answer is figured as follows: $107,000 × 25% =$26,750.

82. The answer is C. An executor can only elect to transfer the DSUE amount to the surviving spouse if Form 706 is filed timely; that is, normally within 9 months of the decedent's date of death or, if the estate has received an extension of time to file, before the 6-month extension period ends. The executor handling the estate must file an estate tax return (IRS Form 706), even if no tax is due, in order to take the DSUE election.[23]

83. The answer is D. A high deductible health plan (HDHP) can be combined with a health savings account (HSA) as part of an employer's benefits package. Even if set up by an employer, an HSA account is *owned and controlled* by the employee. Contributions may be made by the employee, the employer, or any other person. Amounts in an HSA may be accumulated over the years or distributed on a tax-free basis to pay for qualified medical expenses.

---

[23] IRS Rev. Proc. 2017-34 offers a simplified method for estates meeting certain requirements to obtain an extension to file an estate tax return and elect portability, but this only applies to estates that are under the filing threshold. In other words, the provision for relief does not apply to an estate that is required to file an estate tax return and files the return late.

84. The answer is A. In assessing the trust fund recovery penalty, the IRS may hold someone responsible who intentionally disregarded the law or was "plainly indifferent" to its requirements. No *malicious or bad motive* is required for the IRS to successfully assess the penalty. In past court cases, the IRS has even assessed the trust fund recovery penalty against volunteer (unpaid) directors.

85. The answer is D. A self-employed taxpayer's first estimated payment is due April 15. The payment dates for individual taxpayers are due as follows:

- January 1 to March 31 payment is due April 15.
- April 1 to May 31 payment is due June 15.
- June 1 to August 31 payment is due September 15.
- September 1 to December 31 payment is due January 15 of the following year.

If the due date for an estimated tax payment falls on a Saturday, Sunday, or legal U.S. holiday, the payment will be timely if it is remitted by the next business day.

> **Note:** Although most self-employed taxpayers must make estimated payments on a quarterly basis, there are special rules for estimated tax due dates for self-employed farmers and fishermen. See the *Form 1040-ES Instructions* for more information about estimated payments.

86. The answer is C. Based on Gracie's business usage, the total *cost* that qualifies for the section 179 deduction is $14,700 ($24,500 cost of van × 60%). Since Gracie uses the van more than 50% for her business, then she may multiply the cost of the van by her actual percentage of business use. The result is the cost of the property that can qualify for the section 179 deduction (this question is modified from an example in IRS Publication 463).

87. The answer is A. If an estate's beneficiary sells inherited property that is a capital asset, the gain or loss is *always* considered *long-term,* regardless of how long the beneficiary held the property. See IRS Publication 559, *Survivors, Executors and Administrators* for more information.

88. The answer is B. The partnership's basis for depreciation is limited to the adjusted basis of the property in Gerardo's hands, $40,000.

89. The answer is D. Exempt entities, regardless of their entity type, would use Form 8868, *Application for Automatic Extension of Time to File an Exempt Organization Return,* to request an automatic extension of time to file.

> **Note:** An exempt entity can be organized as a corporation for *legal* purposes, but for IRS purposes, it is treated as an exempt entity and should always file its annual tax return on Form 990, *Return of Organization Exempt from Income Tax.*

90. The answer is A. Excise taxes are independent of income taxes. In general, an excise tax is a tax imposed on the sale of specific goods or services, or on certain uses. Federal excise tax is usually imposed on the sale of things like fuel, airline tickets, heavy trucks and highway tractors, indoor tanning, wagering and gambling activities, tires, tobacco and other goods and services. Businesses that are subject to excise tax generally must file a **Form 720,** *Quarterly Federal Excise Tax Return,* to report the tax to the IRS.

91. The answer is B. A paycheck issued after the date of death to a taxpayer for work performed prior to death is considered IRD (income in respect of a decedent).

92. The answer is A. A business can't deduct as a theft loss the decline in market value of stock acquired on the open market for investment, even if the decline is caused by accounting fraud or other illegal misconduct by the officers or directors of the corporation that issued the stock. There is an exception to this rule for recognized Ponzi schemes. All of the other examples would be deductible as casualty losses. See Publication 547 for more information on casualty losses.

93. The answer is C. Employers would not use Form 941 to report backup withholding or income tax withholding on non-payroll payments (such as pensions, annuities, and gambling winnings). Employers should use Form 941 to report the following amounts:

- Wages paid to employees.
- Tips employees reported to the employer.
- Federal income tax withheld.
- Both the employer and the employee's share of Social Security and Medicare taxes.
- Additional Medicare Tax withheld from employees' pay.
- Current quarter's adjustments to Social Security and Medicare taxes for fractions of cents, sick pay, tips, and group-term life insurance.
- Qualified small business payroll tax credit for increasing research activities.

Employers should instead report these types of withholding on Form 945, *Annual Return of Withheld Federal Income Tax.*

94. The answer is D. Gregory must file Form 8300 to report this transaction by the 15th day *after* the date the cash transaction occurred. Generally, if a business receives more than $10,000 in cash in a single transaction (or in several related transactions), the business must file Form 8300, *Report of Cash Payments Over $10,000 Received in a Trade or Business.* For the purposes of this filing requirement, *cashier's* checks are treated as *cash,* but personal checks are *not.* This filing requirement only applies to businesses transactions, not the sale of personal-use property. For example, the sale of one's personal vehicle is not a business transaction, so a Form 8300 would not be required, even if it was a cash sale over $10,000. See IRS Publication 1544, *Reporting Cash Payments of Over $10,000* for similar examples and more information.

95. The answer is C. Peachtree Farms should keep records relating to property until the statute of limitations expires for the year in which the business disposes of the property. The records must enable the taxpayer to determine the basis or adjusted basis of the land in order to determine gain or loss when the property is sold. For example, the records should show the purchase price, settlement or closing costs, and the cost of any later improvements to the property.

96. The answer is C. Aaron would calculate his self-employment tax on Schedule SE, and attach it to his Form 1040. Self-employment tax is generally calculated on Schedule SE, regardless of whether a self-employed taxpayer files Schedule C or Schedule F.

97. The answer is A. Employers of farm employees don't usually file Form 941. Agricultural employers generally file Form 943, *Employer's Annual Federal Tax Return for Agricultural Employees,* instead. Most employers who have employees are required to file a Form 941 on a quarterly basis to report wages paid and payroll taxes withheld. However, special rules apply to some employers.

- Seasonal employers don't have to file a Form 941 for quarters in which they have no tax liability because they have paid no wages.
- Employers of household employees don't usually file Form 941. See Publication 926 and Schedule H (Form 1040) for more information.
- Employers of farm employees don't usually file Form 941.

98. The answer is B. A closely-held corporation can qualify as a real estate professional if *more than 50%* of the gross receipts for its tax year came from real property trades or businesses in which it materially participated. See Publication 925, *Passive Activity and At-Risk Rules,* for more information.

99. The answer is B. The sale of a business is usually not a sale of a single asset. Generally, when the sale of a business occurs via an asset sale, each asset is treated as being *sold separately* for determining the overall treatment of gain or loss. Both the buyer and seller involved in the sale of a business must report to the IRS the allocation of the sales price among the business assets. The taxpayer must use Form 8594, *Asset Acquisition Statement*, to provide this information. The buyer and seller should each attach Form 8594 to their federal income tax return for the year in which the sale occurred. For more information about the tax treatment of the sale of a business, see IRS Publication 544, *Sales and Other Dispositions of Assets.*

100. The answer is A. The Work Opportunity Tax Credit (WOTC) is a federal tax credit available to employers who hire individuals from eligible targeted groups with significant barriers to employment or other special needs. Targeted groups include ex-felons, qualified veterans, an individual that is receiving or recently received Temporary Assistance to Needy Families (TANF), and handicapped individuals. For more information, see the Instructions for Form 5884, *Work Opportunity Credit.*

#3 Sample Exam: Businesses

(Please test yourself first; then check the correct answers at the end of this exam.)

1. What type of business is permitted to claim the Employee Retention Credit for wages paid after October 1, 2021?

A. Personal Service Corporations.
B. Recovery startup businesses.
C. Only businesses with fewer than 500 employees.
D. Only businesses with fewer than 100 employees.

2. Nickolas became a limited partner in the Realty Blue Partnership, which does not have any inventory of goods or unrealized receivables, by contributing $12,000 of cash upon formation of the partnership. The adjusted basis of his partnership interest on December 31, 2021, is $21,000, which includes his $15,000 share of partnership liabilities. At the end of the year, Nickolas sells his entire partnership interest to an unrelated party for $10,000 cash. How must Nickolas report this transaction?

A. $4,000 capital gain.
B. $6,000 capital gain.
C. $11,000 capital gain.
D. $19,000 capital gain.

3. Chad wants to transfer assets to a corporation in exchange for a controlling interest in the corporation's stock. Which of the following transfers would create a taxable event for Chad under section 351?

A. The corporation assumes liabilities in excess of the basis of the assets transferred.
B. Chad exchanges depreciated property for 100% of the corporation's stock.
C. Chad exchanges cash for 100% of the corporation's stock.
D. Chad exchanges land for 85% of the corporation's stock.

4. The Fonte Foods Corporation opened its doors on April 1, 2021, and incurred $53,000 of organizational costs in its first year of business. How should these costs be treated?

A. $5,000 can be deducted currently. The remaining $48,000 must be amortized over 180 months.
B. $2,000 can be deducted currently. The remaining $51,000 must be amortized over 180 months.
C. None of the organizational costs are deductible. They must be amortized over 180 months.
D. Organizational costs are deductible only in the year prior to the official start of business for a corporation or a partnership.

5. Which of the following cannot be a shareholder in an S corporation?

A. An estate.
B. A U.S. resident.
C. A nonresident alien.
D. A 501(c)(3) exempt entity.

6. Rossdale and Dawn are friends who decide to purchase a car wash business together. They form an LLC on February 18, 2021, and start doing business immediately thereafter. Absent any elections, how will their business be classified for federal tax purposes?

A. Sole proprietorship.
B. Qualified joint venture.
C. Corporation.
D. Partnership.

7. Alex sold his office building to Cassandra, a real estate investor, who plans to use it as a commercial rental property. Alex was liable for $2,000 in delinquent real estate taxes on the property, which Cassandra agreed to pay as a condition of the sale. Which of the following statements is correct?

A. Cassandra can deduct these taxes as a business expense on her Schedule E.
B. Cassandra must add the $2,000 in taxes to her basis in the property.
C. Alex can deduct these taxes as an expense on his Schedule E because he was the owner of the property when the taxes accrued.
D. The expense must be divided equally between Alex and Cassandra in order to be deductible.

8. The maximum estate tax rate in 2021 is _____?

A. 10%
B. 15%
C. 35%
D. 40%

9. Leonard Smith died on March 5, 2021, leaving an estate valued at $22 million. An estate tax return (Form 706) must be filed. Which of the following items would not be deductible from the gross estate, to figure Leonard Smith's taxable estate?

A. Funeral expenses paid out of the estate.
B. State death taxes paid by the estate.
C. Alimony paid after Leonard's death, payable to his ex-spouse.
D. Debts owed at the time of death.

10. The Sutter Partnership's fiscal year-end is November 30. When is its partnership tax return due?

A. February 15
B. January 15
C. March 15
D. April 15

11. Relay Trucking Corporation is closing all of its business operations. During its final liquidation, the corporation distributes property, a tractor-trailer with a fair market value of $50,000 and an adjusted basis of $19,000, to one of its shareholders, Rowan. The tractor-trailer is encumbered by an existing auto loan of $62,000, which Rowan personally assumes. How much gain (or loss) would Relay Trucking recognize in this distribution?

A. $31,000 gain.
B. $12,000 loss.
C. $43,000 gain.
D. $18,000 loss.

12. Ileana is a self-employed tax preparer who files a Schedule C to report her business income. She decided to rebrand her office this year to a well-known tax franchise, Liberation Tax, and she paid a franchise fee to do so. During the year, Ileana has the following purchases, all of which are 100% business-use. She files on the cash basis. Ignoring any income limitations, what is her section 179 deduction for 2021?

New computer system	$4,600
New multi-line phone system	$3,600
Utility bills for her office	$1,300
Franchise license from Liberation Tax	$23,000

A. $8,200
B. $9,500
C. $31,200
D. $32,500

13. Which of the following events may cause an automatic termination of an S election?

A. One shareholder dies and the shares are now owned by the deceased shareholder's estate.
B. An exempt entity is gifted 5% of the shares from an individual shareholder.
C. The S corporation was previously a C corporation, and it has passive investment income that exceeds 25% of its gross receipts for three consecutive tax years.
D. Due to stock sales, the number of shareholders reaches 100.

14. Selene is the sole beneficiary of a family trust that her father, Isaac, set up before his death. Isaac died on February 20, 2021. The trust is not required to distribute all of its income in any given year. Given the following information related to activity following her father's death, how much income related to the trust must Selene report on her individual tax return for 2021?

Trust Activity	
Taxable income	$27,000
Tax-exempt interest income	$3,000
Distributable net income	$30,000
Required distributions	$15,000
Discretionary distributions	$7,500

A. $15,000
B. $22,500
C. $27,000
D. $30,000

15. Bunter Energy Inc. is a cash-basis C Corporation. Bunter Energy does not have an applicable financial statement. The company purchases six laptop computers in 2021. The company paid $2,000 each for a total cost of $12,000, and these amounts are substantiated with an invoice. The company has a written accounting procedure in place to expense the cost of tangible property. How should this purchase be treated for tax purposes?

A. Bunter Energy Inc. can deduct each computer as an expense without any required election.
B. Bunter Energy, Inc. is required to capitalize and depreciate the computers under MACRS.
C. Bunter Energy Inc. can deduct each computer as an expense if the company makes the de minimis safe harbor election.
D. Bunter Energy, Inc. is required to capitalize and depreciate the computers under the straight-line method.

16. Forman Financial Group, Inc. sets up an individual HSA (Health Savings Account) for all its employees during the year. Forman Financial Group, Inc. will make contributions to the HSA on the employees' behalf, and employees will also be able to contribute part of their salary. Which form must Forman Group file to report its contributions to an employee's HSA?

A. Form 1099-SA.
B. Form 5498-SA.
C. The HSA contributions are reported on the corporation's yearly tax return (Form 1120).
D. The employee is required to report the value of the HSA on his individual return (Form 1040). No other reporting is needed.

17. Caliber Corporation is a large U.S. corporation owned by two unrelated individuals, Ivan and Todd, who also have more than 80% of the combined voting power for five smaller corporations. Ivan and Todd also have identical common ownership within the five corporations in excess of 50% of the total value of the shares.

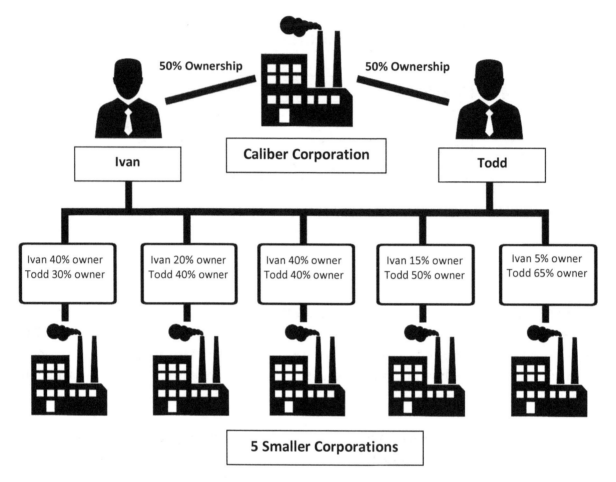

The five *smaller* corporations represent an example of:

A. Personal service corporations.
B. Closely held corporations.
C. A parent-subsidiary controlled group.
D. A brother-sister controlled group.

18. Triad Healthcare, Inc. owns a large medical office building. The company incurred the following expenditures related to the building during the year. Which of the following items does **not** increase the building's basis?

A. The cost of extending new utility service lines to the building.
B. Legal fees related to perfecting title.
C. Assessments for local improvements.
D. Depreciation.

19. Plug-In Corporation is a calendar-year C corporation that manufactures car batteries. Plug-In Corp. had taxable income of $275,000 for the year before figuring their charitable deduction. The company donated $130,000 in cash to several qualified 501(c)(3) charities during the year. None of the contributions were qualified disaster contributions. What is the corporation's allowable deduction for charitable contributions on Form 1120?

A. $13,000
B. $65,000
C. $68,750
D. $130,000

20. Holly contributed an office building to the Naples Partnership in exchange for a 30% partnership interest. The fair market value of the building was $180,000, and Holly's adjusted basis in the building was $60,000 on the date of her contribution. The building was encumbered by a $30,000 mortgage, which the partnership assumed. Based on this information, what is Holly's partnership basis on the date of the contribution?

A. $20,000
B. $30,000
C. $39,000
D. $150,000

21. Caliper Medical Group, Inc. is a cash-basis C corporation and a personal service corporation. The corporation's net income in 2021 is $108,000 before applying a net operating loss carryforward of $22,000 from the previous year. What amount of corporate tax does the company owe in 2021?

A. $18,060
B. $23,000
C. $27,300
D. $30,100

22. Budget Systems, Inc. is struggling to pay its bills. The company's controller, Jessa, decides to pay off creditors by using amounts withheld from the employees' paychecks for income taxes and Social Security taxes, rather than depositing them as required with the federal government. Jessa is not an owner or shareholder of the company, but she is a company officer. Jessa may be subject to which of the following penalties?

A. Late payment penalty.
B. Substantial understatement penalty.
C. Trust fund recovery penalty.
D. Late filing penalty.

23. Which of the following assets is section 179 property?

A. Trademarks
B. Franchise rights
C. Office buildings
D. Fire protection systems

24. Walvis owns a large plot of farmland. In 2021, he foregoes growing his own crops and instead rents the farmland to someone else. The amount of rent Walvis receives is based on the production of the farm by the tenant farmer. After the new tenants arrive, Walvis takes a vacation and is gone for most of the year. Walvis does not materially participate in the farming activity on his farm at all during the year. How should Walvis report this income?

A. Walvis must report the income on Form 4835 as rental income.
B. Walvis must report the income on Schedule E as rental income.
C. Walvis must report the income on Schedule C as ordinary income.
D. Walvis must report the income on Schedule F as ordinary income.

25. Faye is a sole proprietor who operates an airport shuttle service. She owns a minivan she drives herself for business purposes and four additional vans that her employees drive. How should she deduct her mileage for business purposes?

A. She can deduct the standard mileage rate, but she cannot deduct parking fees and tolls.
B. She can deduct the standard mileage rate in addition to related parking fees and tolls.
C. She can choose whether to use the standard mileage rate or deduct actual expenses of operating the vehicles.
D. She cannot use the standard mileage rate. She may deduct the actual expenses of operating the vehicles.

26. The Meza Family Trust had the following income and deductions during the year:

Taxable interest income	$13,000
Capital gains	$3,000
Annual fiduciary fee	$750

Per the trust instrument, capital gains are allocated to income. What is the trust's distributable net income (DNI) for the year?

A. $12,250
B. $13,000
C. $15,250
D. $16,000

27. During the year, the Flusher Partnership distributes $6,000 of cash and factory machinery with an adjusted basis of $15,000 (FMV $23,000) to Antoinette, one of the general partners. Immediately before the distribution, Antoinette's adjusted basis in her partnership interest is $18,000. This was a nonliquidating distribution. What is Antoinette's basis in the factory machinery that was distributed, and what is her remaining partnership basis after the distribution?

A. $5,000 basis in machinery, $9,000 remaining partnership basis.
B. $12,000 basis in machinery, $0 remaining partnership basis.
C. $15,000 basis in machinery, $12,000 remaining partnership basis.
D. $23,000 basis in machinery, $12,000 remaining partnership basis.

28. Which of the following statements regarding distributions from trusts and estates is *incorrect*?

A. Distributable net income (DNI) represents taxable net income before the income distribution deduction.
B. The income distribution deduction is limited to DNI.
C. Beneficiaries must report taxable distributions in the year they are distributed.
D. The amounts taxable to beneficiaries are reported to them on Schedules K-1.

29. Tenley is the sole owner and shareholder in Melcher Associates Inc., a cash-basis S corporation. The company had the following activity during the year:

Gross income from business operations	$50,000
Tax-exempt interest	$1,000
Residential rental income	$5,000
Charitable contribution to a 501(c)(3)	$2,000
Deductible business expenses	$20,000

Based on the above figures, how much "non-separately stated" income must Melcher Associates, Inc. report on Form 1120S?

A. $28,000
B. $30,000
C. $35,000
D. $55,000

30. For a business to deduct meal expenses, which of the following is correct?

A. The meal was paid in cash.
B. The meal resulted in new or expanded business.
C. The meal is an ordinary and necessary business expense.
D. The meal was provided for the benefit of employees.

31. Arian and Marco are both enrolled agents. Together, they formed A&M Tax Solutions, a calendar-year partnership, to provide tax preparation services. Before they began business operations on December 1, 2021, they incurred legal fees of $4,000 and consulting expenses of $1,000 to draft their partnership agreement and file the required forms to trademark their business name. They eventually want to franchise their idea, so they also paid a commission of $600 to a broker to market partnership interests to potential investors. How much of these expenses may be either deducted or amortized?

A. $0
B. $4,000
C. $5,000
D. $5,600

32. Wilson is a 20% shareholder in Lauder Facilities Inc., a C corporation. Wilson has an outstanding $22,000 shareholder loan from the corporation. Wilson files for bankruptcy and defaults on the loan on March 25, 2021. Lauder Facilities cancels Wilson's debt on December 31, 2021. How should this cancellation of debt be reported by Lauder Facilities?

A. Lauder Facilities should report the cancellation as a $22,000 taxable distribution to Wilson.
B. Lauder Facilities can take a deduction for the bad debt.
C. Lauder Facilities should report the canceled debt as a business expense.
D. Lauder Facilities should treat the canceled debt as a $22,000 return of capital.

33. In 2021, Hawaii Sunset Tours purchased a helicopter for $6 million and placed it into service on November 1, 2021. The corporation's taxable income for 2021 was $28 million before figuring any depreciation. What is the business' allowable section 179 deduction and/or bonus depreciation for the helicopter?

A. The company does not qualify for section 179 or bonus depreciation.
B. $0 section 179 deduction; $6 million in bonus depreciation.
C. $2.5 million section 179 deduction; $3.5 million bonus depreciation.
D. $1 million section 179 deduction; $5 million bonus depreciation.

34. Isaak and Javier form Montrose Builders, an equal 50/50 partnership. They plan to offer construction services to the public. Isaak contributes $30,000 in cash, and Javier contributes construction equipment with an FMV of $40,000 and an adjusted basis of $25,000. What is the basis in the partnership of each partner?

A. Isaak has a $30,000 basis, and Javier has a $25,000 basis.
B. Isaak has a $30,000 basis, and Javier has a $40,000 basis.
C. Isaak has a $25,000 basis, and Javier has a $25,000 basis.
D. Isaak has a $27,700 basis, and Javier has a $27,500 basis.

35. Shania owns a bookkeeping and payroll business as a sole proprietor. She has the following income and expenses:

Gross receipts from bookkeeping services	$42,000
Supplies expense	$3,500
Wages paid to a part-time receptionist	$5,000
Utility expenses	$800
Section 1231 gain from the sale of business property	$800
Charitable contribution	$1,200

How much business income should Shania report on her Schedule C?

A. $32,300
B. $32,700
C. $33,500
D. $53,300

36. Which business is not eligible to start a SIMPLE retirement plan for its employees?

A. A business that has union employees.
B. A business that is organized as a corporation.
C. A business that is organized as a partnership.
D. A business that has 110 employees.

37. Trinity Data, Inc. is a cash-basis C corporation. The corporation was formed on May 15, 2021. It elected the calendar year as its accounting period. When is its 2021 corporate tax return due?

A. March 15, 2022
B. April 18, 2022
C. May 15, 2022
D. October 17, 2022

38. Jourdan is an attorney. He transfers an office building worth $125,000 and renders legal services valued at $13,000 to the Beltway Corporation in exchange for stock valued at $138,000. After these transactions, Jourdan owns 95% of the outstanding corporate stock. The remaining 5% of the corporation's stock is owned by an unrelated party. How much gain, income, and/or loss does Jourdan recognize?

A. $13,000 capital loss.
B. $13,000 capital gain.
C. $13,000 ordinary income.
D. No gain or loss is recognized in this transaction.

39. Which of the following is not a pass-through entity?

A. C corporation.
B. S corporation.
C. Sole proprietorship.
D. Partnership.

40. A C corporation generally must make estimated payments throughout the year. For a calendar-year corporation, when are estimated tax payments due?

A. April 15, June 15, September 15, and December 15.
B. March 15, June 15, September 15, and January 15.
C. April 15, June 15, September 15, and January 15.
D. January 15, April 15, June 15, and September 15.

41. Sharon acquires a 20% interest in the Vault Partnership by contributing a factory building that had an adjusted basis to her of $800,000 and is encumbered by a $400,000 mortgage. Vault Partnership assumes the mortgage debt and the payment of the mortgage. The basis of Sharon's partnership interest after this transfer is:

A. $400,000
B. $480,000
C. $640,000
D. $800,000

42. Ten years ago, Tensor Mining, Inc. purchased a plot of undeveloped land for $90,000. On January 5, 2021, the land was condemned by the federal government for development of a new highway. The company attempted to fight the condemnation, but they lost their case in court. On December 19, 2021, Tensor Mining, Inc. receives a $160,000 condemnation award for the land. On February 10, 2022, the company purchases replacement land for $80,000. The rest of the condemnation award was used to purchase inventory. How much gain, if any, should Tensor Mining, Inc. recognize on this event?

A. $0
B. $10,000
C. $70,000
D. $160,000

43. In 2021, Expo Corporation made a nondividend distribution of $2,800 to its sole shareholder, Benton. Benton's stock basis before the distribution was $13,500. What is the effect of this transaction?

A. Benton must report a $2,800 capital gain.
B. Benton must report a $2,800 capital loss.
C. Benton must report a $2,800 ordinary gain.
D. Benton must reduce his stock basis by $2,800.

44. Tabitha is a 5% shareholder in Script Holdings Inc., a C corporation. Tabitha is not an employee of the company; she is only an investor. Script Holdings loans Tabitha $40,000 interest-free for one year. The applicable federal rate at the time of the loan is 4%. She pays the entire loan back by the end of the year, but she does not pay any interest to Script Holdings. How will this transaction be reported, and will Tabitha have to recognize any income?

A. Tabitha must recognize $1,600 of imputed interest as dividend income. The corporation is not allowed a deduction for the dividend paid.
B. Tabitha must recognize $1,600 of imputed interest as dividend income, and the corporation will be allowed a tax deduction for the dividend paid.
C. Tabitha will not be required to recognize any dividend income as long as she repays the loan within the year.
D. Tabitha must recognize $40,000 as taxable income. This type of loan is not permitted by law.

45. The Georgia Literary Association is an organization that fosters literacy programs for children and their parents. Which form should the organization use to apply for formal tax exemption under IRC section 501(c)(3)?

A. Form 990.
B. Form 1023.
C. Form 1024.
D. Literary organizations do not qualify for tax exemption under 501(c)(3).

46. If an S corporation distributes appreciated property (rather than money) to a shareholder, what is the income effect on the corporation?

A. Gains or losses are not recognized because an S corporation is a pass-through entity.
B. Gains are recognized for distributions of appreciated property, but losses are not.
C. Gains are not recognized for distributions of appreciated property, but losses are recognized.
D. Both gains and losses are recognized for distributions of appreciated property.

47. Angie owns a 30% interest in the SportPro Partnership, which is in the business of selling sporting equipment. All the partners share profit and loss according to their ownership interests. There are no limited partners. The SportPro Partnership reports $90,000 of ordinary income for 2021 and distributes $23,000 in cash to Angie. How much income will Angie recognize on her individual return, and what is the character of the income?

A. $23,000 income, subject to self-employment tax.
B. $23,000 income, not subject to self-employment tax.
C. $27,000 income, subject to self-employment tax.
D. $27,000 income, not subject to self-employment tax.

48. Energizer Investments, Inc. is a calendar year, cash-basis C corporation. The company was formed on February 1, and 2021 is the first year that the corporation has been in operation. The corporation has the following items of income and loss during the year:

Short-term capital gain	$30,000
Long-term capital loss	($95,000)

How should this activity be reported on the corporation's Form 1120?

A. The corporation has a $65,000 short-term capital loss carryforward.
B. The corporation has a $65,000 long-term capital loss carryforward.
C. The corporation has a $65,000 net operating loss.
D. The corporation has a $65,000 long-term capital loss carryback.

49. Suzette is a general partner in the Scripps Partnership. Suzette receives a distribution of a parcel of land from the partnership that has a fair market value of $180,000 and a basis to the partnership of $40,000. Her outside basis in the Scripps Partnership was $33,000 prior to the distribution of the land. How will this distribution impact Suzette?

A. She must recognize a capital gain of $7,000, and her basis in the land is $40,000.
B. She must recognize a capital gain of $7,000, and her basis in the land is $50,000.
C. She must reduce her partnership basis to zero, and her basis in the land is $180,000.
D. She must reduce her partnership basis to zero, and her basis in the land is $33,000.

50. Arnold and Harry are brothers. They are equal partners in an LLC that is taxed as a partnership. Two years after forming their LLC, they file Form 8832, *Entity Classification Election*, to elect to be taxed as a C corporation. Shortly thereafter, however, they changed their minds again and decided that they wanted to switch back to a partnership. How long must they wait before they are allowed to change their entity classification again?

A. They must wait five years (60 months) after their corporation election.
B. They must wait at least one year after the date of the corporation election.
C. They must wait at least 180 days after the close of their fiscal year.
D. They can change entity choice at any time simply by filing another Form 8832.

51. Stuart and Kara are father and daughter. Stuart is a 70% partner in the BlueTrack Partnership, and Kara is a 60% partner in the Jupiter Partnership. If the BlueTrack Partnership sells property at a loss to the Jupiter Partnership, what is the result of the transaction?

A. Stuart can deduct his share of the loss on his Schedule K-1.
B. Stuart and Kara can each deduct his or her share of the loss according to their percentage ownership in the respective partnerships.
C. No loss is allowed in the transaction because the partnerships are related parties.
D. The transaction is prohibited and will be disallowed by the IRS.

52. What tax returns, if any, is First Community Church required to file?

- Paid $40,000 of wages to three part-time church employees.
- Received $800 of unrelated business income from Christmas bingo.
- Received $300,000 of donations from parishioners.

A. A church is not required to file a tax return.
B. First Community Church must file payroll tax returns.
C. First Community Church must file payroll tax returns and Form 990-T.
D. First Community Church must file Form 990, Form 941, and Form 990-T.

53. All of the following qualify for a deduction for *depletion* except:

A. Patents.
B. Timber.
C. Gas wells.
D. Mines and natural deposits.

54. Which of the following *may* be deductible as a business expense?

A. A political contribution.
B. Lobbying expenses related to a state election.
C. Repairs to equipment that increase the useful life of an asset.
D. A prepayment penalty on a mortgage for an office building.

55. Axle Foods, Inc. is a fiscal year C corporation that reports income and loss on the accrual basis. Which of the following is required for the company to deduct an expense?

A. Axle Foods must first pay the expense in order to deduct it.
B. Axle Foods must receive an invoice or other bill for an expense in order to deduct it.
C. Axle Foods must have received a bill and paid it before the end of its fiscal year.
D. Axle Foods must meet the "all events" test and have economic performance in order to deduct the expense.

56. Alyson and Ryker are equal partners in a partnership. At the end of the year, prior to any distributions, the adjusted basis of Alyson's partnership interest was $60,000. She received cash of $31,000 as a year-end distribution, plus manufacturing equipment with a fair market value of $38,000 and an adjusted basis to the partnership of $46,000. This was a nonliquidating distribution. What is Alyson's basis in the manufacturing equipment that was distributed to her?

A. $9,000
B. $29,000
C. $38,000
D. $46,000

57. Which of the following entities is *required* to use the accrual method of accounting?

A. A C corporation with average annual gross receipts of $20 million.
B. A partnership with average annual gross receipts of $15 million.
C. An S corporation with average annual gross receipts of $30 million.
D. An LLC with average annual gross receipts of $24 million. The business carries inventory.

58. DeLuca Properties, Inc. initiates a like-kind exchange of an office building. DeLuca Properties must *identify* the property to be received within <u>how many days</u> after the date the company transfers the property given up in the exchange?

A. 30 days.
B. 45 days.
C. 60 days.
D. 180 days.

59. Of the following examples, which asset is a section 1250 property?

A. Copyright.
B. Tractor.
C. Factory building.
D. Racehorse.

60. Driveline Technology, Inc. is a calendar-year S corporation. Driveline has four shareholders. The corporation has 10,000 shares outstanding. The shareholders have the following ownership:

Shareholder		Ownership
1.	Thomas	4,500 shares
2.	Ashley	2,000 shares
3.	Simon	2,000 shares
4.	Charlotte	1,500 shares
Total Shares		**10,000 shares**

Charlotte and Thomas wish to terminate Driveline Technology's S election in order to become a C corporation, but Ashley and Simon do not. Which of the following statements is correct?

A. Charlotte and Thomas do not have enough stock ownership to terminate the election.
B. All of the shareholders must agree to terminate an S election.
C. Charlotte and Thomas have enough stock ownership to terminate the election.
D. At least 75% of the shareholders with active ownership must agree to the termination.

61. Guaranteed payments are made to partners and are determined without regard to the partnership's income. When are guaranteed payments included in an individual partner's taxable income?

A. Guaranteed payments are included in a partner's income in the year they are distributed.
B. Guaranteed payments are taxable when declared by the partnership.
C. Guaranteed payments are not included in a partner's income.
D. Guaranteed payments are included in income in the partner's tax year in which the partnership's tax year ends.

62. Hackett sells vegetables and flowers in the downtown Farmer's Market, which operates five days a week. Hackett grows the flowers and vegetables in a greenhouse behind his home, which he uses exclusively for business. The greenhouse is a separate structure from his home. Hackett is a farmer, so he files a Schedule F to report income and loss. How should the costs of the greenhouse be treated on his tax return?

A. Hackett can deduct the cost of the greenhouse and the expenses for its use.
B. Hackett cannot deduct the cost of the greenhouse because it is not a qualifying structure.
C. Hackett can only deduct a portion of the greenhouse because it is built on his personal property.
D. Hackett should deduct the costs of the greenhouse on Schedule E.

63. The Tucker Partnership has three equal partners: Carlton, Diana, and Cheri. Carlton doesn't want to continue working in the business, so Diana and Cheri agree to let him liquidate his partnership interest. On December 31, Carlton receives a cash distribution of $20,000 in exchange for his entire partnership interest. The partnership has no section 751 assets. Carlton's partnership basis at the time of the distribution was $12,000. How would this transaction be reported by Carlton?

A. $8,000 capital gain.
B. $8,000 in ordinary income.
C. $12,000 in capital gain.
D. $20,000 capital gain.

64. LaFrance Cosmetics, Inc. gives each of its traveling salespeople $1,000 a month ($12,000 a year) as an automobile and travel allowance. The salespeople do not have to provide any proof of their expenses to LaFrance Cosmetics. How should these payments be treated?

A. The allowances are deductible as a fringe benefit, and they are not taxable to the employees.
B. LaFrance Cosmetics must include $12,000 on each salesperson's Form W-2. The amounts are not subject to Social Security or Medicare tax.
C. LaFrance Cosmetics must include $12,000 on each salesperson's Form W-2. The amounts are subject to Social Security and Medicare tax.
D. The auto allowance can be treated as a nontaxable employee fringe benefit.

65. Deroche Consulting, Inc, a C corporation, rents office space from its only employee-shareholder, Scarlett. The fair rental value of the office space is $4,500 per month, but Deroche Consulting pays Scarlett $6,000 per month, and the corporation deducts the full amount as rent expense. Which of the following statements is correct?

A. The IRS may reclassify $4,500 per month of rental payments as a constructive dividend.
B. The IRS may reclassify $1,500 per month of rental payments as a constructive dividend.
C. The IRS may reclassify $6,000 per month of rental payments as a constructive dividend.
D. The IRS may reclassify $1,500 per month of rental payments as a stock dividend.

66. Rodd is a professional securities broker/dealer. His business, Riverside Brokerage, Inc. is organized as an S corporation. Rodd is the sole shareholder in the S corporation. He is unmarried and files as Single. In 2021, Rodd's taxable income, before any potential QBI deduction, is $378,000. Is he eligible for the 199A 20% deduction for Qualified Business Income (QBI)?

A. No, he is not eligible.
B. Yes, he is eligible.
C. He is eligible for a partial deduction.
D. Not enough information to answer.

67. On October 1, 2021, Spillway Corporation, a cash-basis, calendar-year corporation, purchases land with an existing foundation with a $200,000 cash down payment and an existing mortgage of $300,000. Spillway also pays attorneys' fees of $23,000 to complete the purchase and clear legal title to the property. Spillway demolishes the existing foundation and clears the land to start construction of a new building. The demolition costs are $120,000. What is the basis of the land, and how much can be taken as a current expense?

A. $500,000 land basis; $143,000 current expense.
B. $523,000 land basis; $120,000 current expense.
C. $620,000 land basis; $23,000 current expense.
D. $643,000 land basis; $0 current expense.

68. Pumpkin Ranch Farms is a cash-basis C Corporation. During the year, Pumpkin Ranch Farms starts having financial trouble and eventually liquidates. In the course of liquidation, Pumpkin Ranch distributes $10,000 of cash and a tree-cutting machine with a fair market value of $12,000 and an adjusted basis of $8,000 to Randy, a 20% shareholder. Randy's basis in his stock is $17,000. How much gain will Randy recognize in this transaction?

A. $2,000
B. $3,000
C. $5,000
D. $18,000

69. Winston and Greta are married. Winston dies on April 3, 2021, with an estate valued at $10 million. Winston did not make any taxable gifts during his lifetime. Greta is named Winston's executor in her late husband's will, and she would like to elect portability. Which of the following statements is true, regarding Winston's estate?

A. An estate tax return (Form 706) is required to be filed for Winston's estate in order to make a portability election.
B. An estate tax return is not required to be filed for Winston's estate in order to make a portability election because the value of his estate is less than the exemption amount. The portability election can be made on a gift tax return (Form 709).
C. An estate tax return (Form 706) is not required to be filed for Winston's estate. Greta can make the portability election on her individual tax return, as long as she files jointly with Winston in 2021.
D. An estate tax return (Form 706) is not required to be filed for Winston's estate. Greta should file Form 1041 to make a portability election.

70. Omicron Energy, Inc. has $260,000 of current and accumulated earnings and profits. Omicron Energy had no accumulated earnings and profits at the beginning of the year. The company distributes a parcel of land with a fair market value of $200,000 and a basis of $90,000 to Aldo, an 80% shareholder. This is not a liquidating distribution. How much gain (or loss) would the corporation have in this transaction, and how much dividend income would Aldo report on his individual return?

A. Omicron Energy: $110,000 gain. Aldo: $90,000 dividend.
B. Omicron Energy: $110,000 gain; Aldo: $200,000 dividend.
C. Omicron Energy: $200,000 gain; Aldo: $110,000 dividend.
D. Omicron Energy: $200,000 gain. Aldo: $170,000 dividend.

71. Some partnerships and S corporations may have to file Schedule K-2 and Schedule K-3 in 2021. What are Schedules K-2 and K-3 used for?

A. Schedules K-2 and K-3 are used to report international tax information.
B. Schedules K-2 and K-3 are used to report hot assets.
C. Schedules K-2 and K-3 are used to report political contributions.
D. Schedules K-2 and K-3 are used to disclose tax shelter activities.

72. Shaun is a 10% partner in the Tumbleweed Partnership. On December 31, his partnership basis, prior to any distributions, was $7,000. During the year he received a distribution of $10,000 in cash, plus a car with a partnership basis of $3,000 and a fair market value of $4,500. What are the results of these transactions to Shaun, and how must he recognize the distributions?

A. $3,000 of capital gain; his partnership basis is zero; and his basis in the car is zero.
B. $6,000 of capital gain; his partnership basis is zero; and his basis in the car is $3,000.
C. Zero of capital gain; his partnership basis is ($3,000); and his basis in the car is $3,000.
D. $4,500 of capital gain; his partnership basis is zero; and his basis in the car is $4,500.

73. Marley decides to invest in Bally Power, Inc., a cash-basis C corporation, as a new shareholder. In exchange for 70% of the corporation's total stock, he exchanges a business building with an adjusted basis to him of $360,000 and a fair market value of $700,000. Based on this information, what is Marley's stock basis and his recognized gain on the exchange?

	Marley's Stock Basis	Recognized Gain
A.	$360,000	$0
B.	$340,000	$360,000
C.	$700,000	$238,000
D.	$700,000	$340,000

74. Which of the following is not a shareholder loss limitation for an S corporation?

A. Debt basis limitation.
B. At-risk limitation.
C. Passive activity loss limitation.
D. Casualty loss limitation.

75. Liam is the sole shareholder of Shadow Brook Corporation. During the year, Shadow Brook sells a utility van with an adjusted basis of $12,000 and a fair market value of $22,000 to Liam's sister, Gayle, for $11,500. Gayle plans to use the utility van in her own business. How must this transaction be reported by the corporation?

A. Shadow Brook has a deductible loss of $500 on the sale of the asset.
B. Shadow Brook has gain of $500 on the sale of the asset.
C. Shadow Brook will not recognize gain or loss on the sale of the asset.
D. Shadow Brook has a deductible loss of $10,500 on the sale of the asset.

76. The section 199A deduction is based on a percentage of Qualified Business Income (QBI). Which of the following types of income is considered "Qualified Business Income"?

A. Short-term capital gains.
B. Rental income from a trade or business activity.
C. Gains from foreign currency transactions.
D. Guaranteed payments to a partner.

77. A four-member LLC is formed during the year. For federal tax purposes, the LLC can make an *election* to be taxed as which of the following?

A. As a C corporation
B. As a partnership
C. As a Qualified Joint Venture
D. As a grantor trust

78. Nicola is the sole shareholder of Heartland Inc., which is a calendar-year, accrual-basis C corporation. On December 31, 2021, Heartland Inc. had accrued a $20,000 bonus for Nicola and $32,000 of wage expenses for other employees. The wages and the bonus were not actually paid until January 5, 2022. How much of these expenses (if any) can Heartland, Inc. deduct on its 2021 tax return?

A. $0
B. $20,000
C. $32,000
D. $52,000

79. What annual tax return must be filed by a bankruptcy estate?

A. A bankruptcy estate does not file a tax return.
B. Form 709.
C. Form 1041.
D. Form 706.

80. Catalina Surfboards, Inc. is a new C corporation that elects to amortize its organizational costs. Which of the following is considered a qualifying organizational cost?

A. State incorporation fees.
B. Costs for issuing and selling stock or securities.
C. The cost of transferring assets to the corporation.
D. The cost of broker's commissions for selling corporate stock.

81. When can legal expenses incurred during a complete liquidation of a corporation be deducted?

A. On the final corporate return.
B. In the year they are incurred.
C. In the year they are accrued or incurred.
D. The liquidation expenses of a corporation are not deductible.

82. Archer Foods, Inc. initiates a section 1031 exchange of 300 acres of farmland (adjusted basis $300,000) for a food processing plant (FMV $1,750,000). Archer Foods, Inc. pays an additional $400,000 in cash to complete the exchange. After the exchange is completed, what is Archer Foods' basis in the processing plant?

A. $300,000
B. $700,000
C. $1,150,000
D. $1,350,000

83. Greta is a U.S. citizen. Her father, Armand, is a majority shareholder in a shoe manufacturing corporation in Germany called Birkenshoes. In 2021, Armand gifts a portion of his stock in Birkenshoes directly to his daughter, Greta. For IRS purposes, Birkenshoes is considered a controlled foreign corporation (CFC). What percentage of stock ownership would force Greta to file a Form 5471, *Information Return of U.S. Persons With Respect To Certain Foreign Corporations?*

A. 5% stock ownership.
B. 10% stock ownership.
C. 50% (or greater) stock ownership.
D. 80% (or greater) stock ownership.

84. Robin invests $1,000 in the Dayton Partnership at the beginning of the tax year in return for a 20% general partnership interest. She materially participates in the business activity. The Dayton Partnership takes out a $500,000 loan to purchase equipment and consequently incurs $100,000 of losses during its first year of operations. What is Robin's basis in the partnership after the end of the partnership's first year, and how should she treat the loss?

A. $20,000 nondeductible loss; $101,000 basis.
B. $20,000 deductible loss; $0 basis.
C. $20,000 nondeductible loss; $0 basis.
D. $20,000 deductible loss; $81,000 basis.

85. Lindsey is a managing member of Charter Electric, LLC, where she provides 2,160 hours of services to the LLC for the year. Charter Electric is treated as a partnership for tax purposes. She has a 50% ownership interest and shares profits and losses based on that percentage. At the beginning of the year, the basis of Lindsey's LLC interest is $35,000. Charter Electric has an $82,000 net <u>ordinary loss</u> for the year. Lindsey's amount at-risk in the LLC at the end of the year is $97,500. How much of this loss can Lindsey use on her tax return against other income sources?

A. $0
B. $6,000
C. $35,000
D. $41,000

86. Which of the following is the IRS likely to consider an "abusive" trust?

A. Creating a nongrantor trust solely for the benefit of a disabled individual.
B. Distributing funds to a charitable organization at the end of a period specified by the trust.
C. Forming a trust that claims depreciation deductions for a taxpayer's personal residence.
D. Transferring assets into a trust that cannot be revoked after it is created.

87. Which of the following properties is not eligible for the section 179 deduction?

A. Livestock.
B. Qualified improvement property.
C. Off-the-shelf computer software.
D. Inventory.

88. John Lincoln dies on March 1, 2021. John owned many valuable assets, and his estate must go through probate. The Lincoln Estate has two beneficiaries, Gwendolyn and Lilia, who are John's adult daughters. On December 31, 2021, the estate distributes $34,000 in cash to Gwendolyn and $14,000 in cash to Lilia. Which form is required to report these distributions to the beneficiaries?

A. Form 1099-DIV.
B. Schedule K-1.
C. Form 1099-NEC.
D. Form 706.

89. Emile is a 100% shareholder in Templeton Devices, Inc., a calendar-year S corporation. On January 1, Emile's stock basis in Templeton Devices was $95,000. Templeton Devices reported the following income and loss during the year:

Ordinary losses from business operations	$15,000
Long-term capital gains	$4,000
Short-term capital losses	$9,000
Municipal bond interest income	$2,000

What was Emile's stock basis in Templeton Devices, Inc. at the end of the year?

A. $73,000
B. $77,000
C. $87,000
D. $95,000

90. Kassandra died on December 31, 2021. At the time of her death, she had not received $15,000 of wages from her employer or $4,000 of rental income from a duplex she owned. A couple of weeks after her death, Kassandra's sole heir, her son Mateo, received checks for the wages and the rent. He deposited the checks into his own bank account. How should Mateo treat this income?

A. Since Mateo received the funds as an inheritance; they are not taxable to Mateo.
B. This income must be reported on Kassandra's final tax return (Form 1040), not on Mateo's.
C. This is income in respect of a decedent. Mateo must include $19,000 of IRD in his gross income. IRD is always treated to favorable capital gains rates.
D. This is income in respect of a decedent. Mateo must include $19,000 of IRD in his gross income. The income will retain its character as ordinary income for the wages and as passive activity rental income.

91. Which of the following types of exempt organizations is always required to file an annual information return (Form 990 or 990-PF)?

A. A church.
B. A governmental unit.
C. A private foundation.
D. A private religious high school.

92. An employer is required to withhold the 0.9% Additional Medicare Tax from any employee who has earned income of more than _____ in 2021, regardless of the employee's filing status.

A. $150,000
B. $200,000
C. $250,000
D. $300,000

93. A 501(c)(3) corporation has $1,400 in unrelated business income. How should this income be reported?

A. The entity should report the unrelated business income on Form 1120.
B. The IRS will revoke the exempt status of a charitable organization if it has business income.
C. The entity should report the unrelated business income on Form 990-T.
D. The entity should report the income on Form 990.

94. Bethany and Allen are long-time business partners in a general partnership. There are no other owners in the business. Allen dies suddenly on September 18, 2021, and Bethany takes over Allen's former ownership in the business following his death, per their partnership agreement. When is the final partnership tax return due (not including extensions)?

A. January 31, 2022.
B. December 15, 2021.
C. January 18, 2022.
D. March 15, 2022.

95. A fire destroyed a storage building owned by Telecast Corporation, and the company received $45,000 as insurance reimbursement. The adjusted basis of the unit was $20,000, and the FMV at the time of the casualty was $50,000. Telecast spends $41,000 of the insurance proceeds on purchasing a new storage building. What is Telecast's taxable gain (or loss) from this involuntary conversion?

A. $4,000 gain.
B. $5,000 loss.
C. $9,000 gain.
D. No gain or loss is recognized.

96. Which of the following entities is NOT subject to the passive activity loss rules?

A. A trust.
B. An estate.
C. A closely held corporation.
D. A partnership.

97. Sherman operates Kroger Farms, LLC as a sole proprietorship and has the following income and expenses in 2021:

Sales of grain and produce	$2,000,000
Sales of market livestock raised on the farm	$200,000
Crop insurance proceeds	$150,000
Rental income from land (based on production of sharecropper-tenant)	$100,000
Proceeds from the sale of used farm machinery	$24,000
Car and truck expenses	($100,000)
Depreciation expense	($700,000)
Fertilizer and other supplies	($500,000)
Contribution to SEP-IRA	($25,000)
Utilities on the farm	($200,000)
Repairs to farming equipment	($100,000)

Based on the information above, what amount of net farm profit (or loss) should be reported on Sherman's Schedule F?

A. $750,000
B. $820,000
C. $850,000
D. $874,000

98. Villaseca Corporation experienced financial difficulties and is going through a complete liquidation. Alejandro, a 20% shareholder, receives a liquidating distribution of property (a diesel truck). Villaseca Corporation's basis in the truck is $12,000, and its fair market value is $52,000. However, the truck is encumbered by a liability of $60,000 (an unpaid auto loan), which Alejandro personally assumes. How much gain would the corporation recognize, and what is the amount of Alejandro's liquidating distribution?

A. $40,000 taxable gain to corporation; $60,000 liquidating distribution to Alejandro.
B. $48,000 taxable gain to corporation; $48,000 liquidating distribution to Alejandro.
C. $48,000 taxable gain to corporation; $0 liquidating distribution to Alejandro.
D. $40,000 taxable gain to corporation; $0 liquidating distribution to Alejandro.

99. Sarsen Tree Farms is a timber farm. The business purchased a number of assets in 2021. Which of the following is not a §1231 asset for the business (assuming all assets are held more than one year)?

A. Purchase of land for growing timber.
B. Machinery and equipment used to process cut trees.
C. Lumber inventory.
D. Permanent land improvements.

100. Unlike limited partners, general partners have _____ for a partnership's debt obligations.

A. Joint and several liability.
B. Limited responsibility.
C. Legal absolution.
D. Nonrecourse liability.

Please review your answer choices with the correct answers in the next section.

Answers to Exam #3: Businesses

1. The answer is B. Only recovery startup businesses can claim the Employee Retention Credit for wages paid after October 1, 2021. The Employee Retention Credit is a refundable tax credit against certain employment taxes equal to 50% of the qualified wages an eligible employer pays to employees.[24] The Employee Retention Tax Credit is a refundable tax credit designed to encourage employers to keep employees on their payroll.

2. The answer is A. Nickolas realizes $25,000 from the sale of his partnership interest ($10,000 cash payment + $15,000 liability relief). He must report **$4,000 as a capital gain** ($25,000 amount realized - $21,000 basis). The sale of a partner's interest in a partnership usually results in capital gain or loss. The gain (or loss) is the difference between the amount realized and the adjusted basis of the partner's interest in the partnership. If the selling partner is relieved of any partnership liabilities, that partner must include the liability relief as part of the amount realized.

3. The answer is A. If liabilities assumed by the corporation exceed the basis of the assets transferred, the relief from liabilities in excess of basis is treated as boot and will result in gain based on the excess of liabilities over basis. In the case of a section 351 exchange, in general, a taxpayer will not recognize any gain or loss on the transfer as long as the following conditions are met:

- The taxpayer receives only stock in exchange for the property, and
- The taxpayer has a controlling interest in the corporation immediately after the exchange. In order to qualify, the taxpayer must have at least 80% ownership in the corporate stock.

4. The answer is B. The Fonte Foods Corporation exceeded the $50,000 threshold for deductible organizational costs by $3,000, so it must reduce its immediate deduction by this amount. The business can deduct **$2,000** of its organizational costs ($5,000 maximum allowable deduction minus the excess of $3,000) immediately. The remaining amount of organizational costs, **$51,000** ($53,000 - $2,000 allowable deduction), must be amortized over 180 months, starting in the month it commences business. Although business start-up and organizational costs are generally capital expenditures, a business can elect to deduct up to $5,000 of business start-up and $5,000 of organizational costs.

5. The answer is C. Shareholders in an S corporation must be U.S. citizens or U.S. residents. A nonresident alien cannot hold shares in an S corporation. All of the other taxpayers are permitted to be shareholders in an S corporation. Corporate shareholders (except for S corporation shareholders that meet the qualified subchapter S subsidiary rules) and partnerships are not eligible S corporation shareholders. However, certain trusts, estates, banks, and tax-exempt corporations, most notably 501(c)(3) corporations, are permitted to be shareholders.

---

[24] The CARES Act authorized the Employee Retention Credit in March 2020. The Consolidated Appropriations Act of 2021 extended the ERC credit into the first and second quarters of 2021. The American Rescue Plan Act of 2021, enacted March 11, 2021, further extended the Employee Retention Credit to eligible employers for wages paid during the third and fourth quarters of 2021. However, the Infrastructure Investment and Jobs Act, enacted on November 15, 2021, retroactively amended section 3134 of the Internal Revenue Code to limit the Employee Retention Credit only to wages paid before October 1, 2021, unless the employer is a recovery startup business.

6. The answer is D. Rossdale and Dawn's car wash business will be classified as a partnership for tax purposes. A limited liability company (LLC) is an entity formed under state law by filing articles of organization as an LLC. A domestic LLC with at least two members that does *not* file Form 8832 is classified as a partnership for federal income tax purposes.

7. The answer is B. Cassandra cannot deduct the taxes as a current expense since they are delinquent real estate taxes, and the person who is legally liable for the debt is Alex. However, the taxes may be added to the property's basis and depreciated as part of the purchase price since Cassandra intends to use the property as a rental. Alex cannot deduct the taxes because he didn't pay them, since Cassandra agreed to pay them as a condition of the sale. If a taxpayer agrees to pay the delinquent real estate taxes that the seller owes on real property, the buyer must treat those taxes as part of the asset's basis. The buyer cannot deduct them as taxes.

8. The answer is D. The estate tax is a tax on the transferred assets of a deceased person to his or her beneficiaries. The maximum estate tax rate is 40% in 2021. For decedents who died in 2021, up to $11,700,000 in assets may be sheltered from the estate tax.

9. The answer is C. Alimony paid after a taxpayer's death would not be deductible from the gross estate to arrive at the taxable estate. These types of payments would merely be treated as distributions to a beneficiary. Once the gross estate has been calculated, certain deductions (and in special circumstances, reductions to an asset's value) are allowed to determine the taxable estate. Deductions from the gross estate may include:

- Funeral expenses paid out of the estate.
- Administration expenses for the estate (if not deducted on Form 1041).
- Debts owed at the time of death.
- Property taxes accrued at the time of death
- The marital deduction (the value of the property that passes from the estate to a surviving spouse who is a U.S. citizen).
- The charitable deduction (the value of the property that passes from the estate to qualifying charities).
- The state death tax deduction (any inheritance or estate taxes paid to any state. Some states impose a death tax, and some do not).

The following items are <u>not</u> deductible from the gross estate:

- Federal estate taxes paid.
- Alimony paid after the taxpayer's death. These payments would be treated as distributions to a beneficiary.

10. The answer is A. The Sutter Partnership's tax return is due on the fifteenth day of the third month *after* the end of the tax year, so that means that the Sutter Partnership's return would be due February 15.

Note: Most partnerships operate on a calendar year, so their due date is March 15. Partnerships may be granted an extra six-month extension of time to file, so a calendar-year partnership generally has an extended due date of September 15.

---

11. The answer is C. Relay Trucking Corporation would recognize a gain of **$43,000** ($62,000 debt relief - $19,000 basis). During a liquidation, a corporation will recognize gain or loss on distributions of non-cash assets. In general, the gain or loss on a liquidating distribution is calculated by subtracting the basis of the property from the fair market value on the date of the distribution (FMV - basis = gain/loss). However, if the property is encumbered by a liability, the gain or loss may have to be adjusted to reflect the assumption of the liability. If the liability is *greater* than the FMV of the property, the amount of the liability is treated as the FMV of the property for purposes of the gain/loss calculation. In this scenario, the loan amount exceeded the FMV of the asset, so the amount of the loan (rather than the FMV) was used in the calculation of the gain or loss.

12. The answer is A. The answer is $8,200. The amount is calculated as follows:

New computer system	$4,600
New multi-line phone system	$3,600
Total qualifying section 179 purchases	**$8,200**

Section 179 applies only to certain asset purchases. The utility bills would be a regular business expense, not a section 179 item. The franchise license is not a section 179 expense. The cost of intangible personal property, including franchise rights, licenses, and similar assets must generally be amortized over 15 years. Intangible assets are also called "section 197 assets."[25] Other examples of intangible assets include:

- A patent, copyright, or formula.
- A license, permit, or other right granted by a governmental unit or agency (such as a liquor license).
- A covenant not to compete associated with the acquisition of an interest in a trade or business.
- Any franchise, trademark, or trade name.

13. The answer is C. An S corporation that was previously a C corporation cannot have passive investment income that exceeds 25% of its gross receipts for three consecutive tax years without putting its status as an S corporation in jeopardy. An S corporation may have a shareholder that is an estate, and some exempt entities (notably 501(c)(3) charities) may own stock in an S corporation. An S corporation can have up to 100 shareholders. Note that some combination of shareholders can potentially be counted as one shareholder for purposes of the 100-shareholder limit for S corporations if they meet certain family relationships to each other. For example, a husband and wife can be treated as a single shareholder.

14. The answer is B. Since she is the trust's sole beneficiary, Selene must report **$22,500** ($15,000 + $7,500), the sum of the required and discretionary distributions she received. The beneficiary of a trust that is required to distribute all its income currently must report the entire share of DNI, *whether or not* she actually received all the distributions during the tax year. The beneficiary of a trust that is not required to distribute all its income currently must report all income that is required to be distributed to her currently (whether or not actually distributed), plus all other amounts paid, credited, or required to be distributed to her, up to her share of distributable net income. A portion of this income is related to the tax-exempt interest earned by the estate, and will therefore not be taxable income to Selene. The tax-exempt interest must be reported on Selene's tax return, regardless of whether or not it is taxable.

---

[25] The IRS designates certain assets as intangible assets under Section 197 of the Internal Revenue Code. This includes most intangible business assets, like intellectual property, goodwill, franchise rights, and similar assets.

15. The answer is C. Bunter Energy Inc. may treat each computer as an expense and deduct the cost in the current year if the company elects the *de minimis safe harbor* on their 2021 return.[26] Businesses may elect to apply a de minimis safe harbor to amounts paid to acquire or produce tangible property used in a trade or business. To make this election, a statement must be attached to the return for the tax year when qualifying assets were purchased. The de minimis safe harbor election does not include amounts paid for inventory or land. See IRS Publication 535, *Business Expenses,* for more information.

16. The answer is B. Form 5498-SA, is used to report HSA contributions (when funds are added to the HSA). Form 1099-SA is used to report HSA *distributions* (when funds are withdrawn). A health savings account (HSA) is a medical savings account that offers tax-free distributions to pay for current medical expenses. HSAs allow taxpayers to save money for medical expenses on a tax-free basis. The HSA account is owned by the individual employee, but contributions to the HSA may be made by an employer or the employee. The employee's own HSA contributions are either tax–deductible or pre-tax (if made by payroll deduction).

17. The answer is D. The diagram is an example of a "brother-sister controlled group." A brother-sister controlled group involves a situation in which five or fewer individuals, estates, or trusts own 80% or more of the combined voting power for multiple corporations, and have more than 50% identical common ownership within the individual corporations. In contrast, a parent-subsidiary controlled group involves a parent corporation that owns at least 80% of the voting power of at least one other corporation (with possible additional corporations that are at least 80% owned by either the common parent or one of the subsidiary entries).

18. The answer is D. Depreciation will decrease an asset's basis. All the other items listed will increase an asset's basis (see chart below, a full list can be seen in Publication 551, Basis of Assets).

Increases to Basis	Decreases to Basis
Capital improvements	Section 179 deduction
Assessments for local improvements	Depreciation
The cost of extending utility service lines	Amortization
Impact fees	Casualty and theft losses and subsequent insurance reimbursements.
Legal fees for perfecting title	Rebates
Zoning costs	Easements

[26] IRS Notice 2015-82 states that for businesses *without* an applicable financial statement (or AFS), the *de minimis safe harbor* threshold is $2,500 for the business to deduct certain tangible property as an expense (rather than depreciate the property). Businesses that issue an applicable financial statement (those that are audited, are required to be issued to the U.S. Securities and Exchange Commission, or another federal or state government agency) may use the same *de minimis safe harbor* procedure to deduct amounts up to $5,000 per invoice or item. A written accounting policy *is* required for taxpayers with an applicable financial statement.

19. The answer is C. The allowable charitable deduction in 2021 for Plug-In Corporation is **$68,750** = ($275,000 × 25%). The CARES Act increased the limit for charitable contributions to 25% of taxable income for corporations for 2021. This increased limit applies only to cash donations and donations of food inventory. Donations of other property are subject to a 10% limit. Like individual taxpayers, corporations are allowed to carry forward charitable contributions that exceed the percentage limits for up to five years. After five years, any unused charitable deduction is lost.

20. The answer is C. An individual partner's basis is increased by her share of partnership debt and decreased by the amount of debt relief. Since Holly was a 30% partner, she retains a corresponding share of the debt. The answer is calculated as follows:

Beginning basis (her adjusted basis in the building)	$60,000
Mortgage debt assumed by the partnership	(30,000)
Holly's share of the debt ($30,000 × 30%)	9,000
Holly's basis in her partnership interest	**$39,000**

21. The answer is A. The corporate tax rate is a flat 21%. This includes personal service corporations. The answer is calculated as follows: ($108,000 - $22,000 NOL) × 21% = **$18,060.**

22. The answer is C. Jessa could be liable for the trust fund recovery penalty. If a company does not remit their income tax withholding and withheld Social Security taxes, the IRS can pursue its collection from officers, directors, stockholders, or any employees that can be held liable for the trust fund recovery penalty. The trust fund recovery penalty (also called the "100% penalty") can be assessed upon anyone found to be responsible for collecting or remitting withheld income and employment taxes and who willfully fails to collect or remit them. The responsible person (or persons) must have either intentionally disregarded the law or been plainly indifferent to its requirements. The amount of the penalty is equal to the unpaid balance of the trust fund tax.

23. The answer is D. The TCJA expanded the definition of section 179 property to allow the taxpayer to elect to include the following improvements made to *nonresidential* real property:

- Qualified improvement property, (which means non-structural improvements to a building's interior).
- Roofs, HVAC, fire protection systems, alarm systems, and security systems.

Answers "A" and "B" are incorrect because section 179 property does not include "intangible" property, such as trademarks, copyrights, or franchise rights (although there is an exception for off-the-shelf computer software). Answer "C" is incorrect because buildings cannot be deducted under section 179.

24. The answer is A. Walvis must report the income on Form 4835. Form 4835 is used by landowners who rent their farmland and receive a part of the crop as their rental payments (this is also called "sharecropping"), but who are not in the business of farming. A landowner is allowed to report on Form 4835 only if he does not materially participate in the farm business. If the landowner is actively involved in running the farm, he would report income and expenses on Schedule F.

25. The answer is D. Faye cannot use the standard mileage rate because she operates five or more vehicles at the same time, which the IRS considers a "fleet of vehicles." Faye is allowed to deduct actual costs (such as gasoline, repairs, etc.). A business may also not use the standard mileage rate if it:

- Claimed a depreciation deduction on the car using any method other than straight-line.
- Claimed a section 179 deduction on the car.
- Claimed the special depreciation allowance on the car.
- Claimed actual car expenses for a vehicle that was leased.

A taxpayer who uses the standard mileage rate or actual costs can also deduct parking fees and tolls (but *not* parking tickets!).

26. The answer is C. Distributable net income is income that is "currently available" for distribution. In this case, it is **$15,250**, or the sum of the trust's interest income and capital gain *minus* the fiduciary fee ($13,000 + $3,000 - $750). Depending on how a trust is written, capital gains may be allocated to income or to the trust's corpus. In the latter case, capital gains would not be included in DNI.

27. The answer is B. Antoinette's basis in the factory machinery is **$12,000**. After the distribution, her partnership basis would be reduced to zero. In a nonliquidating distribution, Antoinette's basis in the partnership must first be reduced by the cash distribution ($6,000). Her basis in the machinery then would be the lesser of:

- Her remaining basis in the partnership, or
- The partnership's adjusted basis in the machinery.

The answer is calculated as follows:

Antoinette's starting partnership basis	$18,000
Reduced by the cash distribution	(6,000)
Lesser of: $12,000 remaining basis or the partnership's basis in the property	**$12,000**

28. The answer is C. A beneficiary of a simple trust or an estate that is required to distribute all its income currently must generally report his share of the income required to be distributed currently, *whether or not* the distribution was received. If the income required to be distributed currently to all beneficiaries exceeds the trust or estate's DNI, each beneficiary must report his proportionate share of the DNI. The determination of whether trust income is required to be distributed currently depends on the terms of the trust instrument and applicable local law. A beneficiary of a complex trust or an estate that is not required to distribute all its income currently must report the sum of:

1. The amount of the income required to be distributed currently (whether or not actually distributed), or if the income required to be distributed currently to all beneficiaries exceeds DNI (without taking into account the charitable deduction), his proportionate share of DNI, and
2. All other amounts properly paid, credited, or required to be distributed, or if the sum of the income required to be distributed currently and other amounts properly paid, credited, or required to be distributed to all beneficiaries exceeds the DNI, his proportionate share of the excess of DNI over the income required to be distributed currently.

29. The answer is B. The company's *non-separately stated* income is calculated as follows ($50,000 - $20,000 business expenses = **$30,000 of "ordinary" income**). The tax-exempt interest and rental income are "separately stated income," and the charitable contribution is also a separately stated item that is not used to figure the S corporation's income. The charitable contributions deduction is taken by the individual shareholder (Tenley) on her individual return (Schedule A, Form 1040[27]). In this respect, the S corporation is similar to a partnership in its tax treatment of charitable contributions.

> **Note**: Do **not** confuse this treatment with charitable contributions of a C corporation. A C corporation is allowed to deduct a limited amount of charitable contributions directly from its taxable income, but an S corporation cannot. Any charitable contributions made by an S corporation flow through to its shareholders for them to potentially deduct on their own returns.

30. The answer is C. Meal expenses are deductible if they are "ordinary and necessary" business expenses. A business is allowed to deduct meals that are incurred while conducting business with a current or prospective client, customer, vendor or employee, as long as recordkeeping requirements are met. In 2021, businesses can deduct 100% of meal expenses paid to restaurants as long as the business owner (or an employee of the business) is present when food or beverages are provided and the expense is not lavish or extravagant. The 100% deduction also applies to per diem meals. All other meals would still be subject to the prior 50% limit. This temporary increase was passed as part of the *Consolidated Appropriations Act of 2021.*

31. The answer is C. A&M Tax Solutions may choose to either deduct or amortize the amounts for legal fees and consulting expenses ($4,000 + $1,000 = $5,000) as organizational expenses. However, the amount paid in commissions to a broker to market partnership interests must be capitalized and cannot be amortized or deducted. The costs for marketing and issuing interests in the partnership such as brokerage, registration, legal fees, and printing costs are syndication costs that are not deductible or amortizable.

32. The answer is A. The cancellation of debt would be a **$22,000** taxable distribution to Wilson. If a corporation cancels a shareholder's debt without repayment by the shareholder, the amount canceled is treated as a taxable distribution to the shareholder. A corporate distribution to a shareholder is generally treated as a distribution of earnings and profits. The distribution would not be deductible as a business expense by the corporation.

33. The answer is B. Hawaii Sunset Tours is not allowed to take a Section 179 deduction for the helicopter, because its total asset purchases for the year exceed the maximum section 179 spending cap "ceiling" for business asset purchases. However, the helicopter purchase is eligible for 100% bonus depreciation.

34. The answer is A. Isaak's basis in his partnership interest is the cash he contributed ($30,000), and Javier's basis is his adjusted basis in the property he contributed ($25,000). The FMV does not affect the basis of the partner's interest. The basis of a partnership interest is the money (cash) plus the adjusted basis of any property the partner contributed.

---

[27] For 2021 most individuals who take the standard deduction can deduct up to $300 ($600 MFJ) of charitable contributions without having to itemize on Schedule A.

35. The answer is B. The answer is calculated as follows:

Gross receipts	$42,000
Supplies expense	(3,500)
Wages paid to a part-time employee	(5,000)
Utility expenses	(800)
Shania's Business income	**$32,700**

The amounts for the section 1231 gain and the charitable contributions are not reported on Schedule C. Section 1231 gains and losses are netted against each other in the same manner as capital gains and losses (for example, the gains and losses from a stock sale), except that a net section 1231 gain is normally considered a capital gain, while a net section 1231 loss is treated as an ordinary loss. The section 1231 gain would be reported on Form 4797. The charitable contributions would be reported on Schedule A if the taxpayer itemizes their deductions.

36. The answer is D. To establish and maintain a SIMPLE retirement plan, a business must have had 100 or fewer employees during the preceding year who received $5,000 or more in compensation during the preceding year. If the business has had a SIMPLE plan for more than a year and then exceeds the 100-worker limit, it can have a two-year grace period to establish a different retirement plan.

37. The answer is B. Trinity Data, Inc.'s 2021 tax return is due April 18, 2022. This short period return covers the accounting period from May 15, through December 31. In general, C corporation tax returns (except those with a June 30 fiscal year end) are due on the fifteenth day of the fourth month after the end of the corporation's taxable year.

> **Note:** April 18, 2022 is the deadline for 2021 corporate tax returns due to the Emancipation Day holiday in Washington DC.

38. The answer is C. The corporation does not recognize any income or loss from this exchange. However, Jourdan (now the majority shareholder) must recognize ordinary income of **$13,000** as payment for services he rendered to the corporation. If a taxpayer transfers property (or money) to a corporation in exchange for stock and immediately gains control of the corporation, the exchange is usually not taxable. This nonrecognition treatment does not apply when a person exchanges *services* for *stock*.[28]

39. The answer is A. A C corporation is taxed as a separate entity and does not have the characteristics of a pass-through entity. Income that is passed through to the shareholders does not retain its character, and it is taxed twice: first at the corporate level when initially earned by the corporation, and second at the shareholder level, generally through taxable dividend distributions to the shareholders. In contrast, partnerships, S corporations, and sole proprietorships are all pass-through entities. For example, a partnership is not a taxpaying entity when filing its tax returns. Each partner reports its distributive share of the partnership's income, gain, loss, deductions, and credits on its own income tax returns and these items generally retain the character that applied to them at the entity's level.

---

[28] In order for a transfer to qualify for nonrecognition treatment under IRC section 351, immediately after the exchange, the transferor must own at least 80% of all other classes of the corporation's stock.

40. The answer is A. A calendar-year corporation's tax year ends December 31. Therefore, its estimated tax payments are due on April 15, June 15, September 15, and December 15. Generally, a corporation must make installment payments if it expects its estimated tax for the year to be $500 or more during the year. See IRS Publication 542, *Corporations,* for more information.

41. The answer is B. The basis of Sharon's partnership interest is $480,000, calculated as follows:

Adjusted basis of contributed property	$800,000
Minus: Part of mortgage assumed by other partners (80% × $400,000)	($320,000)
Basis of Sharon's partnership interest	**$480,000**

If contributed property is encumbered by a liability, or if a partner's liabilities are assumed by the partnership, the basis of the contributing partner's interest is reduced (but not below zero) by the liability assumed by the other partners. Sharon must reduce her basis because the assumption of the liability is treated as a distribution of money to her. The assumption of the liability by the other partners is treated as contributions by them of money to the partnership.

42. The answer is C. Tensor Mining must recognize a gain of **$70,000** ($160,000 - $90,000), because only $80,000 of the $160,000 condemnation award was reinvested in "like" property. If property is condemned (or disposed of under the threat of condemnation), gain or loss is figured by comparing the adjusted basis of the condemned property with the net condemnation award. Gain is recognizable to the extent of the lesser of the amount above or the portion of the award that was not reinvested by the time-frame requirements for involuntary conversions. Since the corporation did not use the entire condemnation award to repurchase similar property, then a portion of the gain must be recognized. The fact that the company purchased inventory is irrelevant.

43. The answer is D. Benton must reduce the basis of his stock by **$2,800**. A nondividend distribution is a distribution that is not paid out of the earnings and profits of a corporation. A nondividend distribution reduces the basis of the shareholder's stock. It is not taxed until the basis in the stock is fully recovered. When the basis of the stock has been reduced to zero, any additional nondividend distribution that is received must be reported as a capital gain.

44. The answer is A. Tabitha will be forced to recognize **$1,600 of imputed interest** as dividend income. When a corporation makes an interest-free loan (or a below-market loan) to a shareholder, the imputed interest is deemed to be a taxable dividend.[29] The corporation is not allowed to take a deduction for the imputed dividends that were paid. However, if the loan is made to an employee, the treatment of the imputed interest is different. When an employer makes an interest-free loan or a below-market loan to an employee, then the imputed interest is considered taxable wage compensation to the employee and is deductible by the employer.

45. The answer is B. A literary organization may qualify for tax-exempt status under section 501(c)(3) of the Internal Revenue Code. In order to apply for recognition of exempt status, the Georgia Literary Association must use Form 1023, *Application for Recognition of Exemption.*

---

[29] There is a notable exception in the law for "de minimis" loans to shareholders. A corporation can make *de minimis* loans of $10,000 or less to shareholders without the payment of interest. The de minimis exception is outlined in IRC §7872.

46. The answer is B. Gains are recognized for distributions of appreciated property, but losses are not. The amount of gain is calculated as if the S corporation had sold the property to the shareholder at its fair market value. Even though both are pass-through entities, this is one instance in which an S corporation differs from a partnership. In the case of a partnership, gains from appreciated property distributed to a shareholder are generally deferred. With an S corporation, however, the gains must be recognized upon distribution.

47. The answer is C. Angie must include **$27,000** (30% × $90,000) in her gross income for the year, in spite of having only received a $23,000 distribution. A partner pays tax on income that is *earned* by the partnership, even if it is not *distributed* to them. A general partner's share of partnership trade or business income is considered income from self-employment and is subject to self-employment tax.

48. The answer is A. Energizer Investments, Inc. has a $65,000 short-term capital loss carryforward. The corporation has a net short-term capital gain of $30,000 and a net long-term capital loss of $95,000. The short-term gain offsets some of the long-term loss, leaving a *net* capital loss of $65,000. When a net capital loss is carried to another tax year, it is treated as a short-term loss (the loss does not retain its original identity as long term or short term). A corporation can carry its short-term losses back three years. However, since 2021 is the first year of the corporation's existence, then the entire loss would be carried forward to the next tax year.

49. The answer is D. Suzette must reduce her basis in the partnership interest to zero. She will have a **$33,000** basis in the land. A partner cannot have a negative partnership basis; so instead, her basis in the land is reduced from $40,000 to $33,000. She does not recognize any income from this transaction and will defer any gain on the land until she sells it. Note that if Suzette had received cash *instead* of property, she would have been forced to recognize a gain of $7,000.

50. The answer is A. Once a business entity makes an election to change its classification, it cannot change the election again within five years (60 months). An election to change an LLC's classification cannot take effect more than 75 days prior to the date the election is filed, nor can it take effect later than 12 months after the date the election is filed. The 60-month limitation does not apply if the previous election was made by a newly-formed eligible entity and was effective on the date of formation.

51. The answer is C. Stuart and Kara are related parties, so their two partnerships are *also* related parties, so the loss is not allowed. Losses will instead be suspended until the property is eventually disposed of in a non-related party transaction. The basis of each partner's interest in the partnership is decreased (but not below zero) by the partner's share of the disallowed loss. If the purchaser later sells the property to an unrelated party, only the gain realized that is greater than the loss not allowed in the original related-party purchase will be taxable.

> **Note:** For the purposes of this rule, two partnerships in which the same person or persons own, either directly or indirectly, <u>more than</u> a 50% capital interest in both partnerships would be considered a related party. So, for example, if Stuart and Kara had ownership of <u>less than</u> 50% in each partnership, then the related party transaction rules would not apply.

52. The answer is B. First Community Church must file payroll tax returns. Unlike most tax-exempt entities that are required to file Form 990, religious organizations (churches, synagogues, mosques, etc.) are generally not required to file an information return to report their income and loss. Churches are also exempt from payment of federal income tax, and therefore, they are not required to file an application for exemption with the IRS, but many churches still seek a formal exemption. Federal law imposes several reporting requirements on exempt organizations, but the main reporting requirements for churches have to do with employment taxes (if they pay employees) and unrelated business income tax, or UBIT. An exempt organization that has $1,000 or more of gross income from an unrelated business must file Form 990–T. Since First Community Church does not have $1,000 of unrelated business income, it is not required to file Form 990-T, but it is still required to file employment tax returns (the Form 941 series) because it pays employee wages.

53. The answer is A. A patent is not eligible for a depletion deduction because it is not a resource that gets used up physically. Instead, patents must be amortized. *Depletion* is the using up of natural resources by mining, quarrying, drilling, or felling. The depletion deduction allows an owner to account for the reduction of a product's physical reserves. Industries that qualify for the depletion deduction are:

- Mining and timber.
- Oil and gas.
- Geothermal energy producers.
- Other similar industries.

54. The answer is D. Prepayment penalties on a business mortgage are deductible as interest expense. The other items listed cannot be claimed as business expenses. Any type of political contribution, kickback, or bribe is not deductible. In addition, lobbying expenses that are incurred to try to influence legislation are not deductible as a business expense. Repairs to equipment that add value to an asset or increase its useful life are considered improvements and must be capitalized and depreciated.

55. The answer is D. Since Axle Foods, Inc. operates on the accrual basis, it must meet the "all events test" and economic performance must have occurred before deducting the expense. Axle Foods is *not* required to pay the expense first. Under the accrual method of accounting, transactions are accrued as they occur, regardless of when the cash (or another form of payment) is paid or received.

56. The answer is B. In general, a partner's basis in distributed property will be the same as the partnership's basis in the property immediately before the distribution. However, in this case, the distributed property had a basis that exceeded Alyson's remaining partnership interest after the cash distribution. Therefore, her partnership basis is reduced to zero, and the basis of the manufacturing equipment is $29,000 to Alyson.

Starting basis	$60,000
Cash distribution	($31,000)
Remaining basis after cash distribution	**$29,000**

57. The answer is C. An S corporation with average annual gross receipts of $30 million would be required to use the accrual method of accounting. Under the TCJA, most businesses may use the cash method of accounting if they meet the $26 million (in 2021) gross receipts test. This is true even if the business produces inventory. Small business taxpayers meeting the gross receipts test may also choose to either treat inventories as non-incidental materials and supplies or conform to the taxpayer's Applicable Financial Statement (AFS).

58. The answer is B. DeLuca Properties has 45 days to *identify* the property or properties it wishes to purchase during the exchange. A section 1031 exchange allows for the deferral of income on the exchange of business or investment real estate. The process is subject to strict deadlines. In a section 1031 exchange, the property to be received must be *identified* in writing (or actually received) within 45 days after the date of transfer of the property given up. Further, the replacement property in a deferred exchange must be received by the earlier of:

- The 180th day after the date on which the property given up was transferred, or
- The due date, including extensions, of the tax return for the year in which the transfer of that property occurs.

> **Note:** The 45-day deadline cannot be changed or extended by the taxpayer. The deadline is based on calendar days; there are no exceptions for weekends or holidays, although the IRS may make exceptions in the case of presidentially declared disasters.

59. The answer is C. Section 1250 property is *real property* (i.e., real estate). It generally includes buildings (including their structural components), most other permanent structures, and land improvements of general use and purpose. Examples of section 1250 property include residential rental property, factory buildings, and office buildings. Since buildings are generally depreciated using the straight-line method, taxpayers usually receive more favorable treatment of depreciation recapture for section 1250 property versus 1245 property.

60. The answer is C. An S election may be revoked if shareholders holding more than 50% of the stock agree to the termination. Since Charlotte and Thomas own more than 50% of the outstanding stock, they can elect to revoke the S election without permission from the remaining shareholders.

61. The answer is D. Guaranteed payments are included in income in the partner's tax year in which the partnership's tax year ends. For example, for a fiscal-year partnership that ends on July 31, 2021, a calendar year partner would have to report any guaranteed payments on their 2021 tax return, even if they received some (or all) of the guaranteed payments in the prior year.

62. The answer is A. Hackett uses the greenhouse exclusively and regularly in his business, so he can deduct the expenses for its use (subject to certain limitations). A self-employed taxpayer can deduct expenses for a separate free-standing structure, such as a studio, workshop, garage, greenhouse, or barn if the taxpayer uses it exclusively and regularly for his business. The structure does not have to be the taxpayer's principal place of business or a place where the taxpayer meets clients, or customers, as long as it is used *exclusively and regularly* for business.

63. The answer is A. A liquidating distribution of cash for a partner's entire interest in a partnership usually results in capital gain or loss for the partner. The gain or loss is the difference between the amount realized and the adjusted basis of the partner's interest in the partnership. Therefore, Carlton has an **$8,000 capital gain** upon the disposition of his partnership interest ($20,000 - $12,000 = $8,000).

64. The answer is C. Since the employees are not required to substantiate their expenses, the car allowance is treated as part of a "nonaccountable" plan. Under nonaccountable plans, funds received by employees are treated as income. Therefore, LaFrance Cosmetics must include the **$12,000** auto allowance on each employee's Form W-2 because it is taxable as wages. The amounts are subject to income tax withholding, as well as to Social Security and Medicare tax.

65. The answer is B. The IRS may reclassify the excess $1,500 per month of rental payments as a *constructive dividend*, which would make the amount taxable to Scarlett as a dividend, and Deroche Consulting would also lose that amount as a deduction. If a corporation rents property from a shareholder and the rent is unreasonably more than the shareholder would charge an unrelated person to rent the same property, the excessive part of the rent may be treated as a distribution to the shareholder. Other examples of constructive dividends include:

- Excessive compensation.
- When a corporation loans money to its shareholder at a below-market interest rate.
- Reimbursement of shareholders' personal expenses.

Constructive dividends (also called constructive distributions) are usually identified as a result of an IRS audit and assessed during an examination.

66. The answer is A. Rodd is not eligible for the new 199A deduction for Qualified Business Income (QBI). As a professional securities dealer, Rodd's business, Riverside Brokerage, would be considered a "Specified Service Trade or Business," (or SSTB) and therefore subject to a taxable income limitation. For an SSTB, the QBI deduction begins to phase out for single filers at an income of $164,900 and phases out completely at $214,900 in 2021. Since Rodd's taxable income exceeds this phase-out threshold, he is not eligible for the deduction. The following are examples of SSTBs:

- Legal professionals (including lawyers, paralegals, and mediators).
- Consultants.
- Healthcare providers (including veterinarians and nurses).
- Professional athletes, coaches, umpires, team managers, etc.
- Accountants (including CPAs, enrolled agents, and bookkeepers).
- Financial service providers.
- Actuarial science.
- Brokerage services, such as professional stockbrokers and securities dealers (this does not include real estate brokers, however).
- Performing artists (including professional singers, musicians, and actors).
- An SSTB also includes a business where the principal asset of the business is the "reputation or skill" of one or more of its employee or owners. The IRS interpreted this rather narrowly, as a trade or business in which a person receives fees, compensation, or other income for endorsing products or services, (such as celebrity endorsements).

67. The answer is D. *All of the costs* must be added to the basis of the land ($643,000). The original basis of an asset includes:

- The purchase price, including any borrowed money to pay for the property.
- Expenses of making the purchase, such as legal fees or realtor fees.
- Any existing liabilities that the seller assumes (such as delinquent property taxes).

Costs incurred to demolish a building are added to the basis of the land on which the demolished building was located. The costs cannot be claimed as a current deduction.

68. The answer is C. A corporation's treatment of distributions is different during a complete liquidation. In a liquidation, a corporation recognizes gain on appreciated assets and losses on depreciated property. Shareholders may also recognize gain or loss on a corporation's distribution of assets during a liquidation based on the fair market value of the assets distributed versus their basis in the shares of the corporation. In this case, Randy's gain would be calculated as follows:

- $10,000 + $12,000 = $22,000 distribution
- $22,000 - $17,000 stock basis = **$5,000 gain to Randy**

69. The answer is A. An estate tax return (Form 706) is required to be filed for Winston's estate in order for Greta (the surviving spouse) to make a portability election. The portability election, or DSUE ("deceased spousal unused exclusion") must be made on a form 706, even when the filing of an estate return may not otherwise be required.

70. The answer is B. Omicron Energy, Inc. would report a **$110,000 gain** ($200,000 FMV - $90,000 basis). Aldo would report a **$200,000** dividend (the fair market value of the property) as the $200,000 figure is less than his $208,000 share of the corporation's earnings and profits. All distributions of appreciated property would trigger gain recognition for the corporation. The distribution to the shareholder is treated as a sale, and gain is reported on the transaction by the corporation. However, a corporation would not recognize a loss on the distribution of property.

71. The answer is A. Schedules K-2 and K-3 are new for the 2021 tax year. Schedules K-2 and K-3 are required by partnerships and S corporations with items of international tax relevance.

72. The answer is A. Since Shaun received a $10,000 cash distribution when his basis was only $7,000, he must recognize capital gain of $3,000 and reduce his partnership basis to zero. A partner cannot have a negative basis. A partner generally recognizes gain on a partnership distribution only to the extent any money (and marketable securities treated as money) included in the distribution exceeds the adjusted basis of the partner's interest in the partnership. Any gain recognized is generally treated as capital gain from the sale of the partnership interest on the date of the distribution. If partnership property (other than marketable securities treated as money) is distributed to a partner, he generally does not recognize any gain until the sale or other disposition of the property. Unless there is a complete liquidation of a partner's interest, the basis of property (other than money) distributed to the partner by a partnership is its adjusted basis to the partnership immediately before the distribution. However, the basis of the property to the partner cannot be more than the adjusted basis of his interest in the partnership reduced by any money received in the same transaction. In this case, because Shaun's basis in the partnership has already been reduced to zero, his basis in the distributed property is also zero.

73. The answer is D. Transferring property (not cash) to a corporation in exchange for stock can be a taxable event. Since Marley is not "in control" of the corporation after the exchange, he must treat the exchange as a sale. For Section 351 purposes, "control" means ownership of at least 80% of the total stock. Since this transaction does not qualify for Section 351 nonrecognition treatment, Marley must recognize a gain on the transfer, which is treated as a sale. Marley's gain is **$340,000** ($700,000 FMV - $360,000 basis). Marley's basis in his stock is **$700,000** after the exchange.

74. The answer is D. There is no such thing as a "casualty loss limitation." There are four shareholder loss limitations:

- Stock and debt basis limitation.
- At-risk limitation.
- Passive activity loss limitation.
- Excessive business loss limitation.

The fact that a shareholder receives a Schedule K-1 reflecting a loss does not mean that the shareholder is automatically entitled to claim that loss. If a shareholder of an S corporation is allocated an item of loss or deduction, the shareholder must have adequate stock and/or debt basis to claim the loss. Even if a shareholder has adequate stock and/or debt basis to claim an S corporation loss, he must also consider the at-risk and passive activity loss limitations and therefore still may not be able to claim the loss. Furthermore, an S corporation would also be limited to the $250,000 ($500,000 if MFJ) limitation on pass-through entity losses for the year. Note that S corporation shareholders only receive debt basis for loans made directly from the particular shareholder to the corporation.

75. The answer is C. Shadow Brook Corporation will not recognize gain or loss on the sale of the asset. There is no loss recognized in this transaction because this is a sale to a related party. A loss on the sale of an asset to a related party is not allowed unless the distribution is done in a complete liquidation. In this case, related parties include members of a family, including siblings, spouse, ancestors (parents, grandparents), and lineal descendants (children, grandchildren). This list is not exhaustive, and related parties can also be entities. IRC section 267 not only applies to family members, but also includes related businesses, trusts, fiduciaries, and a host of other transactions.

76. The answer is B. Qualified Business Income includes only income from a U.S. trade or business. Rental income will qualify as QBI if it is received from a related trade or business, or if the rental activity itself rises to the level of a "trade or business." Income from foreign currency transactions is not "Qualified Business Income" for the purposes of calculating the QBI deduction. In order for a business owner to claim the QBI deduction, the business must operate as a pass-through entity, and also have qualifying income. QBI does *not* include:

- Capital gains or losses.
- Dividends or interest.
- Annuity payments.
- Gains from foreign currency transactions.
- Reasonable compensation paid to owners.
- Guaranteed payments for services paid to business partners.

77. The answer is A. An LLC with at least two members will be automatically taxed as a partnership (this is its default status) or, upon _election,_ as a corporation (either a C corporation or, if eligible, an S corporation).

78. The answer is D. Since Heartland, Inc. is an accrual-basis corporation, the wages are deductible as they are accrued. The full amount of the wages ($52,000) are deductible in 2021.

79. The answer is C. If the bankruptcy estate has gross income that meets or exceeds the minimum amount required for filing, the trustee must file an income tax return on Form 1041. The bankruptcy estate that is created when an individual debtor files a petition under either Chapter 7 or 11 of Title 11 of the U.S. Code is treated as a separate taxable entity. For more information about bankruptcy estates, see Publication 908, _Bankruptcy Tax Guide._

80. The answer is A. State incorporation fees are considered qualifying organizational costs. The following items are capital expenses that cannot be amortized:

- Costs for issuing and selling stock or securities, such as commissions and printing costs.
- Costs associated with the transfer of assets to the corporation.

A business can potentially take an immediate deduction of up to $5,000 of qualifying _organizational_ costs _and_ $5,000 of qualifying _start-up_ costs in the first year it commences business.

81. The answer is A. The legal expenses incurred during a complete liquidation of a corporation can be deducted on the final corporate return.

82. The answer is B. Archer Foods' basis in the new property is $700,000 (the $300,000 basis of the old property plus the additional $400,000 the company paid to complete the exchange). The FMV of the new property has no bearing on the basis in a section 1031 exchange. If a business trades property in a qualified like-kind exchange and also pays money, the basis of the property received is the basis of the property given up, _increased_ by the additional money paid.

83. The answer is B. If Greta owns more than 10% of the stock in a controlled foreign corporation (CFC), she is required to file Form 5471. A U.S. shareholder that owns at least 10% of a controlled foreign corporation (CFC) is required to file Form 5471 annually. A CFC is a foreign corporation that is owned more than 50% by U.S. shareholders.

84. The answer is D. Robin has a **$20,000 deductible loss**. Her basis is now **$81,000**. The amount of a partnership's loss that a partner is allowed to deduct on her tax return is dependent on the partner's basis in the partnership. In general, a partner cannot deduct losses that exceed her partnership basis. Losses disallowed due to insufficient basis are carried forward until the partner can deduct them in a later year. Robin's share of the partnership liabilities increases her basis to $101,000 ($1,000 cash investment + $100,000 share of the partnership's loan balance [$500,000 × 20%]). Robin can deduct her entire $20,000 share of the loss ($100,000 × 20%) because it does not exceed her basis in the partnership, but her basis in the partnership is reduced to $81,000.

85. The answer is C. Lindsey would report **$35,000** of partnership losses and have a $6,000 loss carryforward. A partner can deduct partnership losses only to the extent of her adjusted basis in the partnership. Since Lindsey's distributive share of the loss exceeds her partnership basis, her basis is reduced to zero, and the remaining loss is carried forward. The answer is calculated as follows:

Loss	$82,000
Lindsey's ownership percentage	x 50%
Lindsey's distributive share of loss	$41,000
Minus her basis	($35,000)
Loss carried forward	**$6,000**

Lindsey's amount at-risk in the LLC is more than her share of the loss, so the at-risk loss limitation will not limit her current year deduction beyond that limited by her basis in the partnership. In addition, because of her activity in the LLC, it will not be considered a passive activity, so the passive loss activity rules will not apply in this situation. Since a partnership is a pass-through entity, partnership losses are never carried back. However, individual partners can use their separate shares of the partnership's business losses to figure their individual NOLs.

86. The answer is C. A trust designed to claim unallowable deductions, such as depreciation on a personal residence, would be considered fraudulent, and the taxpayer would be subject to civil and/or criminal penalties. The other answers describe legitimate types of trusts.

87. The answer is D. Inventory is not eligible for the section 179 deduction. The other assets listed all qualify for section 179 accelerated depreciation.

88. The answer is B. The Lincoln Estate must send out a Schedule K-1 to its beneficiaries to report the distributions the beneficiaries receive. The beneficiaries then use the information on Schedule K-1 to report the income on their personal income tax returns.

89. The answer is B. Emile's year-end stock basis is $77,000. The answer is calculated as follows:

Starting basis	$95,000
Ordinary losses	($15,000)
Long-term capital gain	$4,000
Short-term capital loss	($9,000)
Municipal bond interest income	$2,000
Emile's Year-end stock basis	**$77,000**

In computing stock basis, a shareholder starts with his initial capital contribution to the S corporation (the same as a C corporation). Basis is then increased and/or decreased based on the flow-through amounts from the S corporation. An income item or a contribution will increase stock basis while a loss, deduction, or distribution will decrease stock basis.

90. The answer is D. Mateo must include $19,000 ($15,000 + $4,000) of IRD in his gross income. This is income in respect of a decedent (IRD) and must be included in Mateo's gross income (not on his mother's final tax return). IRD is any taxable income that was *earned* but not *received* by the decedent at the time of their death. IRD is not taxed on the final return of the deceased taxpayer. IRD is reported on the tax return of the person (or entity) that actually *receives* the income. IRD retains the same tax character that would have applied if the deceased taxpayer were still alive. The rental income would be taxed as rental income, and the wages would be taxed as ordinary income. IRD can come from various sources, including:

- Unpaid salary, wages, or bonuses.
- Distributions from traditional IRAs and employer-provided retirement plans.
- Deferred compensation benefits.
- Accrued but unpaid interest, dividends, and rent.
- Accounts receivable of a sole proprietor.

91. The answer is C. A private foundation is required to file an annual information return every year, regardless of income. Private foundations file Form 990-PF. Governmental agencies and churches are generally not required to file an annual information return (Form 990). A school below college level affiliated with a church or operated by a religious order is also exempt from the yearly filing requirement. However, churches and governmental agencies are still required to file employment tax returns (payroll returns) if they have employees.

92. The answer is B. The 0.9% Additional Medicare Tax applies to a taxpayer's earned income (including wages, compensation, and self-employment income) that exceeds certain thresholds. An employer must withhold the 0.9% Additional Medicare Tax from any employee who earns more than $200,000. If the employee and his spouse's combined earnings are less than the $250,000 MFJ threshold, they can apply the overpayment against any other type of tax that may be owed on their income tax return.

93. The answer is C. Form 990-T is used by tax-exempt organizations to report and pay the tax on unrelated business income. Any domestic or foreign tax-exempt organization must file Form 990-T, *Exempt Organization Business Income Tax Return*, if it has gross income from an unrelated trade or business of $1,000 or more.

94. The answer is B. In a two-partner partnership, when a partner dies and the surviving partner becomes the sole owner of the business, the partnership is no longer in existence and a final partnership tax return must be filed. The partnership's tax year ended on the date of termination (the date of Allen's death), September 18. When a partnership is terminated before the end of its regular tax year, Form 1065 must be filed for the short tax year from the beginning of the tax year through the date of termination. A partnership tax return is due two and a half months following the end of the month during which a partnership terminates (the 15th day of the third month *after* the year-end). In this case, the return is due on the fifteenth day of the third month following the month of termination, or **December 15, 2021.**

Note: The partnership can request a 6-month extension in order to file the partnership return during the normal filing season by filing *Form 7004, Application for Automatic Extension of Time to File Certain Business Income Tax.*

95. The answer is A. Telecast has a $4,000 gain from the conversion. The adjusted basis of the property was $20,000, and Telecast received an insurance reimbursement of $45,000. Since Telecast only used $41,000 of the insurance reimbursement on qualifying replacement property, the company would recognize a gain of $4,000 ($45,000 - $41,000), the amount that was not reinvested in "like" property.

96. The answer is D. Partnerships are not subject to the passive loss limitation rules. However, the passive activity rules *are* applied at the *partner* level. Entities subject to the passive activity loss rules are:
- Individual taxpayers.
- Estates and Trusts.
- Closely held C corporations (passive losses may offset active income, but not portfolio income).
- Personal Service Corporations.

Partnerships and S corporations are not subject to the passive loss rules, but the individual partners and shareholders of these entities may be subject on their distributive share. In general, aggregate losses from passive activities are allowed only to the extent of aggregate income from passive activities. Suspended passive activity losses would become deductible in the year of disposal of the entire interest of the passive activity (for example, if an individual has suspended passive losses from an investment asset and then sells the investment, the suspended losses would be recognized upon the disposition of the asset).

97. The answer is A. With the exception of the rental income, the proceeds from the used machinery sale, and the SEP-IRA contribution, all of the items listed above are reportable on Schedule F, resulting in a net farm profit of $750,000.

Sales of grain and produce	$2,000,000
Sales of market livestock raised on the farm	200,000
Crop insurance proceeds	150,000
Rental income from land	NO
Proceeds from the sale of used farm machinery	NO
Car and truck expenses	(100,000)
Depreciation expense	(700,000)
Fertilizer and other supplies	(500,000)
Contribution to SEP-IRA	NO
Utilities on the farm	(200,000)
Repairs to farming equipment	(100,000)
Net Farm Profits:	**$750,000**

Gross income from farming activity includes income from sales of farm products, including livestock raised for sale or purchased for resale. Rent received for the use of farmland is generally rental income, not farm income, and since the rent is based on the productivity of the tenant farmer, it is reported on Form 4835, *Farm Rental Income and Expenses*. Sales of land, depreciable machinery and equipment, and livestock held for draft, breeding, sport, or dairy purposes are reported on Form 4797, *Sales of Business Property*. In the case of a sole proprietorship or partnership, if the owners of the business contribute to their own retirement accounts, they must take the deduction as an adjustment to income on Form 1040.

98. The answer is C. Villaseca Corporation must recognize a **$48,000** gain on the distribution ($60,000 loan - $12,000 basis). Because Alejandro personally assumed the $60,000 loan on the truck, the amount of the distribution for the truck is reduced by the $60,000 loan assumption, resulting in a $0 liquidating distribution to Alejandro. Although the $60,000 liability is treated as the FMV of the truck for calculating gain for the corporation, on the shareholder side, IRC Section 301(b)(2) reduces the amount of the distribution (but not below zero) to the shareholder by the amount of the liability assumed by the shareholder. When property is distributed in a complete liquidation, the transaction is treated as if the corporation sold the assets to a buyer at fair market value. The corporation recognizes gain or loss on the liquidation in an amount equal to the difference between the FMV and the adjusted basis of the assets distributed. Amounts received by the shareholder in complete liquidation of a corporation are treated as full payment in exchange for the shareholder's stock. A liquidating distribution is considered a return of capital and is not taxable to the shareholder until the shareholder recovers his entire basis in the stock. After the basis of the stock has been reduced to zero, the shareholder must report any additional amounts received as a capital gain. If a dissolving corporation distributes property that is subject to a liability, the gain or loss is adjusted to reflect assumption of the liability. If the liability is greater than the FMV of the property, the amount of the liability is treated as the FMV of the property. In this case, because the remaining loan amount is more than the FMV of the truck, the amount of the liability is treated as the truck's FMV.

99. The answer is C. Inventory is not a §1231 asset. Examples of §1231 assets include: land, buildings, land improvements, and equipment and machinery held more than one year. Land improvements are also §1231 assets and depreciable. Examples of land improvements include: fences, roads, and land drainage and irrigation systems.

100. The answer is A. Unlike limited partners, general partners have *joint and several* liability in a partnership's debt obligations. Limited partners are only liable up to the amount of their investment.

About the Authors

Joel Busch, CPA, JD

Joel Busch is a tax professor at San Jose State University, where he teaches courses at both the graduate and undergraduate levels. Previously, he was in charge of tax audits, research, and planning for one of the largest civil construction and mining companies in the United States. He received both a BS in Accounting and a MS in Taxation from SJSU and he has a JD from the Monterey College of Law. He is licensed in California as both a CPA and an attorney.

Christy Pinheiro, EA, ABA®

Christy Pinheiro is an Enrolled Agent and an Accredited Business Accountant. Christy was an accountant for two private CPA firms and for the State of California before going into private practice.

Thomas A. Gorczynski, EA, USTCP

Thomas A. Gorczynski is an Enrolled Agent, a Certified Tax Planner, and admitted to the bar of the United States Tax Court. Tom is also a nationally known tax educator and currently serves as editor-in-chief of EA Journal. He received the 2019 Excellence in Education Award from the National Association of Enrolled Agents. He earned a Master of Science in Taxation from Golden Gate University and a Certificate in Finance and Accounting from the Wharton School at the University of Pennsylvania.

See more information on our official website: *www.PassKeyOnline.com.*

CPSIA information can be obtained
at www.ICGtesting.com
Printed in the USA
BVHW020413150223
658298BV00021B/1018